ACTS 13–28:

A Pentecostal Commentary

Dr. Matthew N. O. Sadiku

Order this book online at www.trafford.com
or email orders@trafford.com

Most Trafford titles are also available at major online book retailers.

Print information available on the last page.

ISBN: 978-1-4907-7644-6 (sc)
ISBN: 978-1-4907-7646-0 (hc)
ISBN: 978-1-4907-7645-3 (e)

Library of Congress Control Number: 2016913589

Trafford rev. 09/09/2016

 www.trafford.com

North America & international
toll-free: 1 888 232 4444 (USA & Canada)
fax: 812 355 4082

CONTENTS

To

My late parents-in-law:
Adedoyin and Samuel Odusote

Other books by the author

Secrets of Successful Marriages
How to Discover God's Will for Your Life
Wisdom: Your Key to Success
Choosing the Best: Living for What Really Matters
Matthew 1-15: A Pentecostal Commentary
Matthew 16-28: A Pentecostal Commentary
Mark: A Pentecostal Commentary
Luke 1-11: A Pentecostal Commentary
Luke 12-24: A Pentecostal Commentary
John 1-11: A Pentecostal Commentary
John 12-21: A Pentecostal Commentary
Acts 1-12: A Pentecostal Commentary
Romans: A Pentecostal Commentary
1 Corinthians: A Pentecostal Commentary
2 Corinthians: A Pentecostal Commentary
Ephesians: A Pentecostal Commentary
Galatians: A Pentecostal Commentary
Philippians and Titus: A Pentecostal Commentary
Colossians and Philemon: A Pentecostal Commentary
1 & 2 Thessalonians: A Pentecostal Commentary
1 & 2 Timothy: A Pentecostal Commentary
1 & 2 Peter: A Pentecostal Commentary
Hebrews: A Pentecostal Commentary
James and Jude: A Pentecostal Commentary
1-3 John: A Pentecostal Commentary
Revelation: A Pentecostal Commentary

PREFACE

Earnest Christians are hungry for information that makes their Bible come alive. The Christian life can be described as getting to know God better each day. Every Christian should regularly—daily read the Word of God. We should find time for quiet or personal devotions. The reason we have so many "bad" days is that we do not spend time with God. We must spend time with God if we want His blessings on our lives and desire to hear from Him.

For over 20 years I have used commentaries in my devotions. The blessings derived from the commentaries are overwhelming. I am writing this commentary to share some of those blessings and lessons I have learned over the years.

This commentary provides verse-by-verse exposition and application on Acts. It is different from others in two respects. First, it is brief while some commentaries are unnecessarily wordy and verbose. This commentary does not delve into critical and exegetical details. Therefore, the limits of this commentary forbid that we consider all the views concerning any issue, but an attempt will be made to provide a brief, sound, yet scholarly view.

Second, it is Pentecostal in outlook. This implies that we generally adhere to the doctrine of biblical inerrancy and adopt a literalist approach to the interpretation of the Bible. Pentecostal doctrines include speaking in tongues, gifts of the Holy Spirit, signs and wonders, divine inspiration, divine healing, to mention but a few. The early church was basically Pentecostal in nature, i.e. it exercised considerable freedom in using the gifts of the Holy Spirit in her life and worship. Although this book is written from a Pentecostal perspective, I draw ideas from scholars from all denominations and hope that the book serves all Christians.

The task of writing a commentary on a verse is similar to what the Amplified Bible does to the verse. If the verse in a regular version is regarded as 100%, the Amplified Bible typically amplifies it 150%, while the commentary typically amplifies it 500%. Thus, the commentary helps you see the verse clearly.

It is not easy to write a commentary on any book in the Bible. In order to provide a readable text, this commentary is based on the New International Version (NIV) translation. The commentary is for laymen, pastors, teachers, and all students of the Word. It is designed to enrich your quiet time or personal study by making the commentary clear and simple. With your Bible in one hand and this commentary in the other, you will be able to unpack the deep truths of God's Word. It is my prayer that this commentary brings you both delight and insight in understanding the Word of God.

I owe a great deal to many scholars whose commentaries on Acts I have consulted. It is my pleasure and honor to thank Dr. David Momoh and Victor Akeredolu for reviewing the manuscript. I owe special thanks to my wife for her support and prayer.

ABBREVIATIONS

AB	Amplified Bible
cf.	confer, compare
ESV	English Standard Version
ibid.	*ibidem*, in the same place
KJV	King James Version
LXX	Septuagint, the OT in Greek
NASB	New American Standard Bible
NIV	New International Version
NKJV	New King James Version
NLT	New Living Translation
NRSV	New Revised Standard Version
NT	New Testament
OT	Old Testament
RSV	Revised Standard Version
TLB	The Living Bible
v., vs.	verse, verses

CHAPTER 1

FIRST MISSIONARY JOURNEY

Acts 13:1-12

Paul and Barnabas Commissioned

Verses 1-3: Now in the church at Antioch there were prophets and teachers: Barnabas, Simeon called Niger, Lucius of Cyrene, Manaen (who had been brought up with Herod the tetrarch) and Saul. ² While they were worshiping the Lord and fasting, the Holy Spirit said, "Set apart for me Barnabas and Saul for the work to which I have called them." ³ So after they had fasted and prayed, they placed their hands on them and sent them off.

1 Luke now moves to the final stage of the witness as outlined by Jesus: witness to the ends of the earth (Acts 1:8). Now in the church at Antioch there were prophets and teachers: Barnabas, Simeon called Niger, Lucius of Cyrene, Manaen (who had been brought up with Herod the tetrarch) and Saul. In Acts 11:27, we are told that some prophets came down from Jerusalem to Antioch, the capital of Syria. Barnabas and Saul were two of those prophets and teachers in Antioch. The other three men (Simeon, Lucius, and Manaen) were not known. Some have suggested that Simeon was nicknamed Niger (Latin for black) because he was a black man. The church was apparently heterogeneous.

Prophets receive revelations from God and foretell the future. The gift of prophecy is the special ability God gives individuals to receive messages from Him and communicate them to His people. Teachers edify and establish believers in the truth. They provide a clear understanding of the Word of God. The gift of teaching is the special ability God gives to

1

individuals to communicate information in such a way that others may learn.

Prophets and teachers are two of the five key offices in the church (Ephesians 4:11). The church at Antioch was a gifted and Spirit-filled church. "A Spirit-filled church may be defined simply as one whose members walk in obedience to the will of God."[1]

2 While they were worshiping the Lord and fasting, the Holy Spirit said, "Set apart for me Barnabas and Saul for the work to which I have called them." A message like this usually comes through a prophet. The message came when they were worshiping and fasting as a group. Jesus expected His disciples to fast (Matthew 6:17). Fasting enables us to do without legitimate things such as food and focus on prayer. It weakens the flesh and strengthens the spirit. Isaiah 58:4-14 tells us what a fasting ought to be. Unfortunately, fasting is much neglected by the church in our time.

3 Barnabas and Saul were set apart, as the Spirit demanded. After the church had fasted and prayed, they placed their hands on them and sent them off. "The church's prayer was accompanied by fasting, both when the church received the message and when they sent off the missionary team (13:2-3)."[2]

The laying on of hands signified identification and unity in purpose. God did the commissioning through the church, through the laying on of hands. God chose the two best men who were actively involved in ministering and committed them to the task of evangelizing the Gentiles. They were the backbone of the local church at Antioch and they would be sorely missed.

Evangelism in Cyprus

Verses 4-7: The two of them, sent on their way by the Holy Spirit, went down to Seleucia and sailed from there to Cyprus. [5] When they arrived at Salamis, they proclaimed the word of God in the Jewish synagogues. John was with them as their helper. [6] They traveled through the whole island until they came to Paphos. There they met a Jewish sorcerer and false prophet named Bar-Jesus, [7] who was an attendant of the proconsul, Sergius Paulus. The proconsul, an intelligent man, sent for Barnabas and Saul because he wanted to hear the word of God.

4 The two of them, Barnabas and Saul, sent on their way by the Holy Spirit, went from Antioch down to Seleucia in Syria and sailed from there to Cyprus. It is the Holy Spirit who is responsible for sending out His servants. Cyprus was an island in the Mediterranean Sea. It was the home of Barnabas (Acts 4:36) and that might account for the reason they started the missionary outreach there. They stayed there for a while.

5 They arrived at Salamis, which was a port city in Cyprus. They proclaimed the Word of God in the Jewish synagogues. John Mark was with them as their helper. As an assistant, Mark was possibly responsible for instructing the new converts and taking care of practical needs. The missionaries established a strategy or pattern they would generally follow in all their missionary outreach. They first went to the synagogue, seeking out people of their own kind.

6 They traveled through the whole island of Cyprus until they came to Paphos, which was a port city and the Roman capital of Cyprus. There they met a Jewish sorcerer and false prophet named Bar-Jesus. Bar-Jesus means "Son of Jesus." Ironically, he opposed God's salvation through Jesus. He also called himself Elymas (v. 8), which means "the enlightened one." This false prophet was a practitioner of magic and the occult. He performed magic to deceive people. Saul and Barnabas encountered this false prophet in Paphos, just as Philip and Peter did in Samaria.

7 Bar-Jesus was an attendant of the proconsul, Sergius Paulus. The proconsul or governor of Cyprus was an intelligent man, indicating that he had sound understanding. He decided to hear the gospel firsthand. He sent for Barnabas and Saul because he wanted to hear the Word of God. He wanted to know more about the new teaching sweeping across Cyprus.

Opposition of Bar-Jesus

Verses 8-12: But Elymas the sorcerer (for that is what his name means) opposed them and tried to turn the proconsul from the faith. ⁹ Then Saul, who was also called Paul, filled with the Holy Spirit, looked straight at Elymas and said, ¹⁰ "You are a child of the devil and an enemy of everything that is right! You are full of all kinds of deceit and trickery. Will you never stop

3

perverting the right ways of the Lord? ¹¹ Now the hand of the Lord is against you. You are going to be blind for a time, not even able to see the light of the sun." Immediately mist and darkness came over him, and he groped about, seeking someone to lead him by the hand. ¹² When the proconsul saw what had happened, he believed, for he was amazed at the teaching about the Lord.

8 But Elymas the sorcerer (for that is what his name means) opposed them and tried to turn the proconsul from the faith. He was afraid that the governor Sergius Paulus might be converted and then he would lose his status. He recognized the threat the gospel would have on his influence. Leading someone to Christ involves engaging in a battle against the forces of the enemy. In this case, Saul and Barnabas battled against Elymas for the soul of the governor.

9 Then Saul, who was also called Paul, filled with the Holy Spirit, looked straight at Elymas. This is the first place in the NT we find the familiar name Paul. Many Jews often had both Jewish and Roman names. Saul in Hebrew means "appointed one," while the Roman name Paul means "little one." As the apostle to the Gentiles started the Gentile phase of his ministry, he would have to go by the Roman name. He was filled with the Holy Spirit indicating that He controlled his ministry from start to finish.

Elymas had been the Roman governor's mentor up to this time. He understood that if the governor believed in Christ, there would be no need for a sorcerer. When Elymas tried to counteract Paul's witness to the governor, Paul fixed his gaze on Elymas, the sorcerer. He would soon expose his wicked ways without apology and without fear

10,11 Saul said to Elymas, "You are a child of the devil and an enemy of everything that is right! You are full of all kinds of deceit and trickery. Will you never stop perverting the right ways of the Lord? Now the hand of the Lord is against you. You are going to be blind for a time, not even able to see the light of the sun." Paul regarded Elymas as the enemy of righteousness. He accused him of perverting the truth of God and being the enemy of goodness and truth. Immediately mist and darkness came over him, and he groped about, seeking someone to lead him by the hand. As Paul indicated, the blindness was only temporary. Perhaps the blindness would lead Elymas to repentance and salvation.

12 When the proconsul saw what had happened, he believed, In other words, when the governor saw Elymas smitten with blindness, he realized that God was with Paul. He was amazed at the teaching about the Lord. The teaching was with signs following. The miracle was all it took to convince the proconsul. "The truth and the power of Christ are united and complement one another. We are responsible for proclaiming the truth, but the manifestation of the power is in God's hand."[3]

NOTES

1. John MacArthur, *The MacArthur New Testament Commentary: Acts 13-28* (Chicago, IL: Moody Publishers, 1996), p. 3.
2. Ajith Fernando, *Acts: The NIV Application Commentary* (Grand Rapids, MI: Zondervan, 1998), p. 374.
3. Derek Carlsen, *Faith & Courage: Commentary on Acts* (Arlington Heights, IL: Christian Liberty Press, 2000), p. 306.

CHAPTER 2

AT PISIDIAN ANTIOCH – PART 1

Acts 13:13-41

Arrival in Pisidian Antioch

Verses 13-15: From Paphos, Paul and his companions sailed to Perga in Pamphylia, where John left them to return to Jerusalem. [14] From Perga they went on to Pisidian Antioch. On the Sabbath they entered the synagogue and sat down. [15] After the reading from the Law and the Prophets, the leaders of the synagogue sent word to them, saying, "Brothers, if you have a word of exhortation for the people, please speak."

13 Having completed their ministry in Paphos in Cyprus, Paul and his companions sailed toward the mainland. They arrived at the city port of Perga in Pamphylia, which was located on the southern coast of Asia Minor. Perga is known today as Antalya.

Here in Perga Paul and Barnabas suffered a setback—John Mark left them to return to Jerusalem. We are not told the reason Mark left Paul and Barnabas. Perhaps the missionary lifestyle was too harsh for him. At this point in his life, he was a victim of his own idealistic expectations. God gave Mark another chance. Later Paul would write, "Get Mark and bring him with you, because he is helpful to me in my ministry" (2 Timothy 4:11).

14 From Perga they went on to Pisidian Antioch, about one hundred miles north of Perga. This Antioch was located in Asia Minor and should not be confused with Antioch in Syria, where Paul and Barnabas started their missionary journey. The area around Antioch was known as Galatia. As usual, on the Sabbath they entered the synagogue and sat down. Since Paul was a trained rabbi, he could be sure of a warm reception in any synagogue.

15 After the reading from the Law and the Prophets, the leaders of the synagogue sent word to them, saying, "Brothers, if you have a word of exhortation for the people, please speak." "The Law and the Prophets" refers to the Scripture. The leaders of the synagogue acknowledged the presence of Paul and Barnabas and referred to them as "brothers." They wanted them to address the congregation if they had something to say. Of course, Paul always had something to say. He had the message of the gospel to present. The opportunity to preach Christ had come.

Source: www.all-creatures.org

The History of Israel

Verses 16-22: Standing up, Paul motioned with his hand and said: "Fellow Israelites and you Gentiles who worship God, listen to me! [17] The God of the people of Israel chose our ancestors; he made the people prosper during their stay in Egypt; with mighty power he led them out of that country; [18] for about forty years he endured their conduct in the wilderness; [19] and he overthrew seven nations in Canaan, giving their land to his people as their inheritance. [20] All this took about 450 years. "After this, God gave them judges until the time of Samuel the prophet. [21] Then the people asked for a king, and he gave them Saul son of Kish, of the tribe of Benjamin, who ruled forty years. [22] After removing Saul, he made David their king. God testified concerning him: 'I have found David son of Jesse, a man after my own heart; he will do everything I want him to do.'

16 Standing up, Paul motioned with his hand and said: "Fellow Israelites and you Gentiles who worship God, listen to me!" Paul's audience consisted of Jews and God-fearing Gentiles, who were eager to hear the Word. He asked them to pay attention to what he was about to say. This is the first recorded message of Paul. The message is similar to those given by Peter (Acts 2:14-36; 3:12-26) and Stephen (Acts 7:2-53).

17 "The God of the people of Israel chose our ancestors; he made the people prosper during their stay in Egypt; with mighty power he led them out of that country." In total control of history, God chose Abraham, Isaac, and Jacob and made an unconditional covenant with them. Jacob and his entire family went to Egypt during the famine. At the appropriate time, God led them out of Egypt.

18 After the Exodus, God endured their conduct in the wilderness for forty years. He put up with their unfaithfulness and constant rebellion. The people walked in idolatry, disobedience, and murmuring. God patiently tolerated Israel during their wilderness wandering as a father bears with a wayward son. He gave them the law through Moses. He fed them with manna. He eventually brought a new generation of Israelites into the Promised Land.

19 God overthrew seven nations in Canaan, giving their land to His people as their inheritance. Deuteronomy 7:1 provides the list of people from seven nations: the Hittites, Girgashites, Amorities, Canaanites, Perizzites, Hivites, and Jebusites. These nations were larger and stronger than Israel. It was not by Israel's power that they conquered the land. It was God who gave them Canaan.

20 All this took about 450 years—400 years of captivity in Egypt, 40 years of wilderness wandering, and 10 years conquering the land. "After this, God gave them judges until the time of Samuel the prophet." God responded to the needs of the people by appointing judges. Samuel was the last judge and the first prophet.

21 Then the people asked for a king. There was nothing wrong in their asking for a king. What was wrong was their motive—they wanted to be like other nations. They rejected God as their King. God gave them Saul son of Kish, of the tribe of Benjamin, who ruled forty years. This is the only place in the Bible where the period of Saul's reign is mentioned. Saul's dynasty was cut short with his death because of his disobedience.

22 After removing Saul, he made David their king. God testified concerning him: "I have found David son of Jesse, a man after my own heart; he will do everything I want him to do." David was a man after God's own heart because he desired to do God's will. Although David was far from being perfect, He embodied all the ideal characteristics of a great king—a shepherd, a soldier, a statesman, and a psalmist.

The Promised Messiah

Verses 23-25: "From this man's descendants God has brought to Israel the Savior Jesus, as he promised. ²⁴ *Before the coming of Jesus, John preached repentance and baptism to all the people of Israel.* ²⁵ *As John was completing his work, he said: 'Who do you suppose I am? I am not the one you are looking for. But there is one coming after me whose sandals I am not worthy to untie.'*

23 From this man's descendants God has brought to Israel the Savior Jesus, as He promised. The Messiah was to be the descendant of David and Jesus was. The fulfillment of OT prophecies about the Messiah proves that Jesus was Israel's long-promised Messiah. Jesus was not only the Messiah, He was the Savior. We all need a Savior from the power of sin and Jesus is the only Savior.

24 Before Jesus started His ministry, John the Baptist cleared the way for Jesus. John was His forerunner and the last OT prophet. The essence of his ministry was preparing for the coming of Christ. He preached repentance and baptism to all the people of Israel. John called the people of Israel to repent and be ready for the coming Messiah. John's message was for all people because everyone needed to repent.

25 John's ministry was known in Antioch. As John was completing his work, he said: "Who do you suppose I am? I am not the one you are looking for. But there is one coming after me whose sandals I am not worthy to untie." John corrected the false assumption that he was the Messiah. He considered himself unworthy to untie Messiah's sandals. He pointed people away from himself to Christ.

Universal Opportunity

Verses 26-29: *"Fellow children of Abraham and you God-fearing Gentiles, it is to us that this message of salvation has been sent. [27] The people of Jerusalem and their rulers did not recognize Jesus, yet in condemning him they fulfilled the words of the prophets that are read every Sabbath. [28] Though they found no proper ground for a death sentence, they asked Pilate to have him executed. [29] When they had carried out all that was written about him, they took him down from the cross and laid him in a tomb.*

26 "Fellow children of Abraham and you God-fearing Gentiles, it is to us that this message of salvation has been sent." All Jews prided themselves in being the children of Abraham, the friend of God. God's salvation in the person of Jesus had come to the Jews and God-fearers in Pisidian Antioch. He had made a universal offer of peace and reconciliation freely and equally to both Jews and Gentiles. Paul appealed for them to have faith in Jesus Christ.

27 The people of Jerusalem and their rulers did not recognize Jesus, yet in condemning him they fulfilled the words of the prophets that are read every Sabbath. Paul blamed the death of Jesus on the Jews in Jerusalem who were involved. For three-and-a-half years, Jesus visited Jerusalem again and again and performed miracle upon miracle. Yet they did not recognize Him. They read the OT prophecies in their synagogue week after week. Yet they did not know Him.

The question that is often asked is: If Jesus is the Messiah as He claimed to be, why didn't the religious leaders recognize Him? The answer is that their hearts were hardened. Their hardening of hearts and their condemnation of Jesus serve to fulfill prophecies.

28 Though they found no proper ground for a death sentence, they asked Pilate to have Him executed. They hated Him without cause. They could not pass a death sentence without the cooperation of the Roman governor Pilate. Even the pagan Roman governor could not find fault with Him (John 18:28, KJV). He was forced by the Jews to crucify Jesus. He gave in to their demands.

29 When they had carried out all that was written about Him, they took Him down from the cross and laid Him in a tomb. Although victims of crucifixion were usually buried in mass grave, Jesus was given a decent burial in a tomb to fulfill Isaiah 53:9. Joseph of Arimathea along with Nicodemus were responsible for the burial (John 19:38, 39). God had sent His only Son. They had killed Him and buried Him. They had done their worst to Him.

The Resurrection of Christ

Verses 30-37: But God raised him from the dead, [31] and for many days he was seen by those who had traveled with him from Galilee to Jerusalem. They are now his witnesses to our people. [32] "We tell you the good news: What God promised our ancestors [33] he has fulfilled for us, their children, by raising up Jesus. As it is written in the second Psalm: "You are my son; today I have become your father.' [34] God raised him from the dead so that he will never be subject to decay. As God has said, "'I will give you the holy and sure blessings promised to David.' [35] So it is also stated elsewhere: "You will not let your holy one see decay.' [36] "Now when David had served God's purpose in his

11

own generation, he fell asleep; he was buried with his ancestors and his body decayed. *³⁷ But the one whom God raised from the dead did not see decay.*

30 While men did their worst by killing and burying Jesus in the tomb, the tomb was not the end of the story. God raised Him from the dead. The greatest proof that Jesus is the Messiah is His resurrection. Jesus Himself foretold it and the religious leaders dreaded to see His words come true. To make sure that He did not rise from the dead, they sealed the tomb and put soldiers there. But Jesus rose from the dead anyway. His resurrection is the heart of the gospel. "For if there is no resurrection of the dead, then Christ must still be dead. And if he is still dead, then all our preaching is useless and your trust in God is empty, worthless, hopeless" (1 Corinthians 15:13,14, TLB).

31 "For many days He was seen by those who had traveled with Him from Galilee to Jerusalem. They are now his witnesses to our people." The evidence of the resurrection was provided by the witnesses. For about forty days after His resurrection, Jesus appeared to His disciples and friends from Galilee on different occasions. On one occasion more than 500 witnesses saw Jesus Christ (1 Corinthians 15:6). Christ's resurrection did not happen in a corner, rather there were hundreds of eye witnesses.

32,33 Paul and Barnabas jointly brought them the gospel. "We tell you the good news: What God promised our ancestors he has fulfilled for us, their children, by raising up Jesus. As it is written in the second Psalm: 'You are my son; today I have become your father.'" God affirms that God fulfilled the promise made by raising up Jesus. The fathers had patiently waited for the promise, but it was their children who lived to see it. Paul found a convincing proof of Jesus' deity in Psalm 2:7. All quotations were from the LXX.

34 God raised Him from the dead so that He will never be subject to decay. Lazarus and Dorcas who were raised from the dead would die again, but not so with Jesus. As God has said, "I will give you the holy and sure blessings promised to David." This is a quote from Isaiah 55:3. The quote promised the sure blessings of David. The eternal throne did not find fulfillment in David, but a seed of David who will reign as eternal King forever.

35 So it is also stated elsewhere: "You will not let your holy one see decay." This is quoted from Psalm 16:10. This is the same messianic psalm Peter quoted in Acts 2:27. In this psalm, David predicted that Messiah's dead body would not be corrupted in the tomb. The Messiah must be killed, buried and resurrected. This is the heart of Paul's message.

36 David served God's purpose in his own generation. He reigned for forty years. During his reign, Israel was raised to the status of a first-class power. Then He fell asleep. He was buried with his ancestors and his body decayed. Psalm 16:10 was surely not fulfilled in David. There David was not speaking about himself but about the Messiah.

37 In contrast to David, the One whom God raised from the dead did not see decay. He did not remain in the tomb. He was raised from the dead with an incorruptible, imperishable body. A dead Messiah serves no purpose. Jesus' body not only escaped decay and corruption, but He also conquered death. He lives forevermore. The Scriptures had been fulfilled in Jesus' suffering, crucifixion, death, burial, resurrection and ascension.

Christ is the Savior

Verses 38-41: "Therefore, my friends, I want you to know that through Jesus the forgiveness of sins is proclaimed to you. *[39] Through him everyone who believes is set free from every sin, a justification you were not able to obtain under the law of Moses.* *[40] Take care that what the prophets have said does not happen to you:*

> *[41] "'Look, you scoffers,*
> *wonder and perish,*
> *for I am going to do something in your days*
> *that you would never believe,*
> *even if someone told you.'"*

38 Therefore, my friends, I want you to know that through Jesus the forgiveness of sins is proclaimed to you. Everyone sins (1 Kings 8:46) and therefore needs forgiveness. We can be set free from the guilt of sin because God laid on Christ the iniquity of us all (Isaiah 53:6).

Ironically, the person they crucified is the One through whom God offers forgiveness of sins. Verses 38 and 39 are the key portion of Paul's message.

39 Through Jesus everyone who believes is set free from every sin, a justification you were not able to obtain under the law of Moses. Keeping the law of Moses cannot free one from sins. The law could condemn and convict a person, but it could not cancel his sin. A man is justified by faith apart from the works of the Law (Romans 3:28). As Warren Wiersbe said, "Justification is the act of God whereby He declares the believing sinner righteous in Jesus Christ."[1]

40,41 Take care that what the prophets have said does not happen to you: "Look, you scoffers, wonder and perish, for I am going to do something in your days that you would never believe, even if someone told you." Paul warns that his listeners should not spurn the offer of salvation. He quotes Habakkuk 1:5, where the prophet warned the people of the impending Babylonian invasion. Paul is solemnly warning his audience about the consequence of rejecting God's provision. "Accepting the salvation offered in Jesus Christ brings forgiveness of sin and eternal bliss. Rejecting it brings judgment and eternal damnation."[2]

NOTES

1. Warren W. Wiersbe, *Be Daring: Acts 13-28* (Colorado Springs, CO: David C. Cook, 1988), p. 18.
2. John MacArthur, *The MacArthur New Testament Commentary: Acts 13-28* (Chicago, IL: Moody Publishers, 1996), p. 27.

CHAPTER 3

AT PISIDIAN ANTIOCH – PART 2

Acts 13:42-52

The Initial Reaction

Verses 42-44: As Paul and Barnabas were leaving the synagogue, the people invited them to speak further about these things on the next Sabbath. ⁴³ When the congregation was dismissed, many of the Jews and devout converts to Judaism followed Paul and Barnabas, who talked with them and urged them to continue in the grace of God. ⁴⁴ On the next Sabbath almost the whole city gathered to hear the word of the Lord.

42 Interest in the gospel was aroused. This was possibly the first time they would hear about Christ. As Paul and Barnabas were leaving the synagogue, the people invited them to speak further about these things on the next Sabbath. The initial reaction of the people to what Paul preached was positive. They wanted to hear more on the next Sabbath. As John MacArthur well said, "For a preacher to so fascinate his listeners that they demand to hear him again is a testimony to the effectiveness of his preaching."[1]

43 When the congregation was dismissed, many of the Jews and devout converts to Judaism followed Paul and Barnabas. While some would wait till the next Sabbath to hear more, some could not wait to hear further instruction. They followed Paul and Barnabas, who exhorted them to continue and persevere in the grace of God. The missionary team must have spent the week ministering to these converts.

15

44 On the next Sabbath, the impact the missionaries had made in the previous week became evident. Almost the whole city gathered to hear the word of the Lord. Those who heard Paul last Sabbath must have informed and invited several others to come and hear Paul and Barnabas. Their contagious enthusiasm brought nearly the whole city to the synagogue. These included both the Jews and Gentiles.

The Jewish Opposition

Verses 45-48: When the Jews saw the crowds, they were filled with jealousy. They began to contradict what Paul was saying and heaped abuse on him. ⁴⁶ Then Paul and Barnabas answered them boldly: "We had to speak the word of God to you first. Since you reject it and do not consider yourselves worthy of eternal life, we now turn to the Gentiles. ⁴⁷ For this is what the Lord has commanded us: "I have made you a light for the Gentiles, that you may bring salvation to the ends of the earth." ⁴⁸ When the Gentiles heard this, they were glad and honored the word of the Lord; and all who were appointed for eternal life believed.

45 When the Jews saw the crowds, one would think that they would rejoice that Gentiles were there to hear about their Jehovah God. Instead they were filled with jealousy. They envied the success of Paul and Barnabas. They had the attitude of the prophet Jonah. "Nothing so infuriated the Jews as the thought that the blessings of salvation might be extended to the despised Gentiles."[2] They had never seen such crowds in their synagogue. They began to contradict what Paul was saying and heaped abuse on him. They opposed Paul's message with abusive talk.

46,47 Paul and Barnabas were not intimidated by the opposition of the Jews. They answered them boldly: "We had to speak the word of God to you first. Since you reject it and do not consider yourselves worthy of eternal life, we now turn to the Gentiles. For this is what the Lord has commanded us: 'I have made you a light for the Gentiles, that you may bring salvation to the ends of the earth.'" It was God's plan that salvation should be first offered to the Jews (Romans 1:16). Unfortunately, some Jews chose to reject the gospel and consequently judged themselves unworthy of eternal life. Because of their rejection, Paul and Barnabas made up their mind to turn to the Gentiles. They looked for an open door. They quoted Isaiah 49:6 to justify their decision. That was a decisive moment in the history of the church.

48 In contrast to Jewish opposition, when the Gentiles heard this, they were glad and honored the Word of the Lord. All who were appointed for eternal life believed. This gives the divine side of evangelism. Believers are saved because God has appointed them for eternal life. They are within the saving purposes of God due to their positive response to the gospel. They have their names written in God's Book of Life (Revelation 21:27).

The Missionaries were Driven from Antioch

Verses 49-52: The word of the Lord spread through the whole region. ⁵⁰ But the Jewish leaders incited the God-fearing women of high standing and the leading men of the city. They stirred up persecution against Paul and Barnabas, and expelled them from their region. ⁵¹ So they shook the dust off their feet as a warning to them and went to Iconium. ⁵² And the disciples were filled with joy and with the Holy Spirit.

49 Luke makes a note of the spread of the Word of the Lord despite the persecution of Paul and Barnabas. The Word of the Lord spread like fire through the whole region. Those who believed Paul and Barnabas shared their faith enthusiastically with others. The whole city of Pisidian Antioch with the surrounding region was turned upside down because the Lord's Word was proclaimed.

50 But unbelieving Jews would not sit back and let Paul and Barnabas take over. They resorted to persecution. The Jewish leaders incited the God-fearing women of high standing and the leading men of the city. They stirred up persecution against Paul and Barnabas, and expelled them from their region. They could drive out the missionaries, but they could not drive out the Holy Spirit who would continue the work.

51 So Paul and Barnabas shook the dust off their feet as a warning to them. This is what Jesus commanded His disciples to do when they suffered rejection (Luke 10:10-12). They went to Iconium, a city which was about eighty miles southeast of Pisidian Antioch. One door closes so that another door may be open. By driving out the missionaries from Antioch, the gospel spreads to other places.

52 Paul and Barnabas left behind two groups of people. On the one hand, there were hate-filled, jealous Jews who rejected the Word. On the other hand, there were joyous, Spirit-filled disciples who accepted the Word. In contrast to the first group who stopped at nothing to get the missionaries out of Antioch, the believers were filled with the loving, forgiving Spirit of God. Paul and Barnabas had to leave their converts, but the Spirit remained with them.

NOTES

1. John MacArthur, *The MacArthur New Testament Commentary: Acts 13-28* (Chicago, IL: Moody Publishers, 1996), p. 32.
2. Ibid., p. 36.

CHAPTER 4

CONFLICT IN ICONIUM

Acts 14:1-7

Paul and Barnabas in Iconium

Verses 1-3: *At Iconium Paul and Barnabas went as usual into the Jewish synagogue. There they spoke so effectively that a great number of Jews and Greeks believed.* *² But the Jews who refused to believe stirred up the other Gentiles and poisoned their minds against the brothers.* *³ So Paul and Barnabas spent considerable time there, speaking boldly for the Lord, who confirmed the message of his grace by enabling them to perform signs and wonders.*

1 Iconium was located in the Roman province of Galatia. Today the city is known as Konya in Turkey. At Iconium Paul and Barnabas went as usual into a Jewish synagogue.

Although they had decided to turn to the Gentiles (Acts 13:46), their returning to the synagogue showed that their strategy remained the same. There they spoke so effectively that a great number of Jews and Greeks (or Gentiles) believed. Their ministry was fruitful and effective because it was done through the power of the Holy Spirit. The Holy Spirit energized the words of the missionaries to produce conviction and conversion.

2 But the Jews who refused to believe stirred up the other Gentiles and poisoned their minds against the brothers. The unbelieving Jews were always a pain in the neck of the missionaries. Having heard the gospel and rejected it, they became bitter enemies of Paul and Barnabas.

Satan used them to poison the minds of potential believers. He is always counteracting the work of God.

3 The opposition did not intimidate Paul and Barnabas. Their courageous attitude showed their loyalty to Christ through thick and thin. They spent considerable time in Iconium, speaking boldly for the Lord, who confirmed the message of His grace by enabling them to perform signs and wonders—possibly healing the sick and driving out demons. The signs and wonders attest to the fact that the missionaries spoke for God.

Paul and Barnabas Driven out of Iconium

Verses 4-7: The people of the city were divided; some sided with the Jews, others with the apostles. ⁵ There was a plot afoot among both Gentiles and Jews, together with their leaders, to mistreat them and stone them. ⁶ But they found out about it and fled to the Lycaonian cities of Lystra and Derbe and to the surrounding country, ⁷ where they continued to preach the gospel.

4 The unbelieving Jews polarized the people of the city. The multitude was divided. A rift developed among the residents of Iconium. Some sided with the unbelieving Jews, others with the apostles. As Lloyd Ogilvie rightly said, "Some people try to divide and conquer; others simply include and conquer."[1] Notice that Luke refers to Paul and Barnabas as apostles. This is the first time in the NT where Paul was called an apostle. Apostles were messengers sent out to witness for Christ and their work is not yet completed. The office of the apostles is not limited to the Twelve, as we can see here.

5 There was a plot afoot among both Gentiles and Jews, together with their leaders, to mistreat them and stone them. They were planning on a violence for the apostles. The Jews wanted to have Paul and Barnabas publicly insulted and stoned to death. The mind-poisoning leaders stimulated the mob against the missionaries. "Stoning was a Jewish form of execution, usually for blasphemy."[2]

6 But Paul and Barnabas found out about the plot and fled from the area to the Lycaonian cities of Lystra and Derbe and to the surrounding country. They had been driven out of two cities back-to-back. Leaving

Iconium was not an act of cowardice but of prudence. It would not be wise to stubbornly remain in a city where they were not wanted. The local assembly was already established. It was necessary to move on to other places where the gospel was needed.

Like Iconium, both the cities of Lystra and Derbe were in the Roman province of Galatia. Lystra was about 18 miles from Iconium. It was the native home of Timothy, his mother Eunice, and grandmother Lois (Acts 16:1; 2 Timothy 1:5). Derbe was about 40 miles southeast of Lystra.

7 In Lystra and Derbe, the apostles continued to preach the gospel in spite of the opposition and persecution from the previous cities. Wherever Paul went, he preached the gospel. In fact, his motto was: "Woe to me if I do not preach the gospel" (1 Corinthians 9:16). "He preached the gospel in Athens, the intellectual capital of the world, and was mocked; he preached the gospel at Jerusalem, the religious capital of the world, and was mobbed; he preached the gospel in Rome, the political capital of the world, and was martyred. But he preached the gospel."[3]

NOTES

1. Lloyd J. Ogilvie, *Acts: The Communicator's Commentary* (Waco, TX: Word Books, 1983), p. 221.
2. John MacArthur, *The MacArthur New Testament Commentary: Acts 13-28* (Chicago, IL: Moody Publishers, 1996), p. 47.
3. John Phillips, *Exploring Acts* (Grand Rapids, MI: Kregel Publications, 1986), p. 278.

CHAPTER 5

MINISTRY IN LYSTRA

Acts 14:8-20

Healing the Lame Man

Verses 8-10: In Lystra there sat a man who was lame. He had been that way from birth and had never walked. ⁹ He listened to Paul as he was speaking. Paul looked directly at him, saw that he had faith to be healed ¹⁰ and called out, "Stand up on your feet!" At that, the man jumped up and began to walk.

8 Luke mainly concentrates on what went on in Lystra; He does not give any information on what happened in Derbe. No mention is made of a synagogue in Lystra. The major event in the city involved the healing of a man who was lame. Paul was possibly speaking in an open-air meeting. The man sat there in the audience listening to Paul. The man's hopeless condition is described in three ways: impotent in his feet, crippled from his mother's womb, and had never walked. The people of the city knew that the man's physical condition could not be cured by the natural means.

9 The lame man listened to Paul as he was speaking. Paul looked directly at him and saw that he had faith to be healed. The preached Word that the man heard from Paul produced faith, which brought healing. Paul had the gift of discernment and could perceive the man's faith to be healed. He saw an opportunity to use his gift of healing and confirm his message with a sign.

10 Paul called out, "Stand up on your feet!" With a loud voice, Paul commanded the man to stand on his feet. At that, the man jumped up and began to walk without ever learning how to. God miraculously healed the man through Paul. It was a dramatic and spectacular miracle. God used the sign to confirm the message of the gospel as presented by the apostles Paul and Barnabas.

The healing of this man is similar to the lame man healed by Peter in Acts 3:2. The miracle confirmed Paul's status as an apostle of Jesus, comparable to the apostle Peter. Here is another example of "power evangelism."

The Missionaries Regarded as Gods

Verses 11-18: When the crowd saw what Paul had done, they shouted in the Lycaonian language, "The gods have come down to us in human form!" ¹² Barnabas they called Zeus, and Paul they called Hermes because he was the chief speaker. ¹³ The priest of Zeus, whose temple was just outside the city, brought bulls and wreaths to the city gates because he and the crowd wanted to offer sacrifices to them. ¹⁴ But when the apostles Barnabas and Paul heard of this, they tore their clothes and rushed out into the crowd, shouting: ¹⁵ "Friends, why are you doing this? We too are only human, like you. We are bringing you good news, telling you to turn from these worthless things to the living God, who made the heavens and the earth and the sea and everything in them. ¹⁶ In the past, he let all nations go their own way. ¹⁷ Yet he has not left himself without testimony: He has shown kindness by giving you rain from heaven and crops in their seasons; he provides you with plenty of food and fills your hearts with joy." ¹⁸ Even with these words, they had difficulty keeping the crowd from sacrificing to them.

11 When the crowd saw what Paul had done, how he had healed the lame man, they shouted in the Lycaonian language, "The gods have come down to us in human form!" The immediate result of the miracle was that it produced emotional response from the crowd. From their perspective, the healing was an indication that gods had descended. Because they spoke in the Lycaonian language, Paul and Barnabas might not understand what was going on.

12 They called Barnabas Zeus, the chief god or father of the gods. They Paul called Hermes, the messenger of the gods, because he was the chief speaker. The Roman names for Zeus and Hermes were Jupiter and Mercury respectively. Paul and Barnabas were elevated as gods just because of the miracle God performed through them. Some missionaries face this danger of deification because of the extraordinary things they can do.

13 The priest of Zeus, whose temple was just outside the city, brought bulls and wreaths to the city gates because he and the crowd wanted to offer sacrifices to them. Because Zeus had visited them, the most appropriate person to offer the sacrifice was the priest of Zeus. Man is incredibly religious and must worship something. People were more concerned about the healers than the gospel. They were wrongly seeking to deify the two messengers that brought the Good News.

14 But when the apostles Barnabas and Paul heard of this and realized what was going on, they were appalled. (This is the second time Paul and Barnabas were called apostles.) They tore their clothes, a common Jewish way of expressing horror or disapproving blasphemy. They rushed out into the crowd and tried to dissuade the people from worshiping them. Their only goal was to bring glory to the Lord.

15 Paul shouted, "Friends, why are you doing this? We too are only human, like you. We are bringing you good news, telling you to turn from these worthless things to the living God, who made the heavens and the earth and the sea and everything in them." All religions involving worshiping gods are worthless and hopeless. Paul was bold enough to tell the Lycaonians that their religious practices were worthless. He urged them to turn from such worthless idols to the living Jehovah God, the Creator of all things—including Zeus and Hermes.

16 In the past, God let all nations go their own way. He allowed all nations to exist and do His permissive will. He turned His back on the nations and permitted them to their own thing. "There was a tolerance on God's part toward sinners who did not have the full revelation of His holy will… Special revelation came only in the Old Testament Scriptures, entrusted to Israel. The pagan nations, in their ignorance, were left to go their own ways, having only generation revelation."[1]

17 Yet God has not left Himself without testimony: He has shown kindness by giving you rain from heaven and crops in their seasons. He provides you with plenty of food and fills your hearts with joy. His goodness is manifested in the good things He allows people to enjoy— the rains, crops, food, and joy. Because of such acts of kindness to the pagan nations, there is no excuse for rejecting the gospel now.

18 Even with these words about the true God, the apostles had difficulty keeping the crowd from sacrificing to them. With great difficulty, the apostles were able to stop the idolatrous ceremony. It was to their credit that they did not allow such to happen. The crowd calmed down until some troublemaking Jews came from Antioch and Iconium.

Paul is Stoned

Verses 19,20: Then some Jews came from Antioch and Iconium and won the crowd over. They stoned Paul and dragged him outside the city, thinking he was dead. ²⁰ But after the disciples had gathered around him, he got up and went back into the city. The next day he and Barnabas left for Derbe.

19 Then some Jews came from Antioch and Iconium and won the crowd over. They were able to convince the crowd that Paul and Barnabas were false prophets. The fickle crowd stoned Paul and dragged him outside the city, thinking he was dead. Stoning was a horrible, painful way of executing criminals. "The influence of the Jews is seen in the stoning, which was their way of executing a criminal."[2] Paul was not really dead. They only supposed or thought he was dead. He would later refer to this occasion (2 Corinthians 11:25). We do not know what they did to Barnabas.

20 But after the disciples had gathered around Paul and undoubtedly prayed for him, he got up and went back into the city. Paul had some converts in Lystra since they had stayed long enough and Timothy was

25

one of them (Acts 16:1). The next day he and Barnabas left for Derbe. Since the door of opportunity to minister closed in Lystra, they moved to another city, Derbe, about 80 miles away. Paul was not deterred by stoning; he was committed to making the most of his time.

NOTES

1. John MacArthur, *The MacArthur New Testament Commentary: Acts 13-28* (Chicago, IL: Moody Publishers, 1996), p. 51, 52.
2. John Phillips, *Exploring Acts* (Grand Rapids, MI: Kregel Publications, 1986), p. 283.

CHAPTER 6

RETURN TO ANTIOCH

Acts 14:21-28

Installing the Elders

Verses 21-25: They preached the gospel in that city and won a large number of disciples. Then they returned to Lystra, Iconium and Antioch, [22] strengthening the disciples and encouraging them to remain true to the faith. "We must go through many hardships to enter the kingdom of God," they said. [23] Paul and Barnabas appointed elders for them in each church and, with prayer and fasting, committed them to the Lord, in whom they had put their trust. [24] After going through Pisidia, they came into Pamphylia, [25] and when they had preached the word in Perga, they went down to Attalia.

21 Paul and Barnabas preached the gospel in that city of Derbe and won a large number of disciples there. After completing their work in Derbe, they returned to Lystra, Iconium and Antioch. They visited the three cities they had just carried out missionary work in. It is hard to imagine how the missionary team went back to enemy territory or places where they had been expelled. This required courage and determination. It seems that their focus on the return trip was different from their first visit. "So God-centered and kingdom-focused was the apostle Paul that he seems to have taken no heed of threats made against his life."[1]

22 Their objective for visiting those cities was to strengthen the disciples and encourage them to remain true to the faith. "We must go through many hardships to enter the kingdom of God," they said. Suffering and persecution are part and parcel of our calling (John 16:33). Our sufferings are somehow linked with Christ's sufferings. "No servant is greater than his master. If they persecuted me, they will persecute you also" (John 15:20). We must expect persecution and not be intimidated by it.

23 For new Christians to survive, they need the care and mentorship of some spiritual leaders. So Paul and Barnabas returned to the churches to organize their leadership. They appointed elders for them in each church. With prayer and fasting, they committed the elders to the Lord, in whom they had put their trust. The fact that the elders were selected after prayer and fasting shows how serious the selection was and that they seriously sought the guidance of the Holy Spirit. The elders would be responsible for taking care of the members after Paul and Barnabas departed. The elders were Spirit-filled men chosen from the local congregation.

24,25 After going through region of Pisidia, Paul and Barnabas came into the region of Pamphylia heading south. Antioch was in Pisidia. But their final destination was Antioch in Syria, where the missionary journey started.

When they had preached the word in Perga which was in Pamphylia, they went down to Attalia. It was at Perga that John Mark disserted the missionary team and headed home. Attalia was close to Perga and it was a seaport. At Attalia, they embarked on a ship for Antioch in Syria.

Completing the First Missionary Journey

Verses 26-28: From Attalia they sailed back to Antioch, where they had been committed to the grace of God for the work they had now completed. ²⁷ On arriving there, they gathered the church together and reported all that God had done through them and how he had opened a door of faith to the Gentiles. ²⁸ And they stayed there a long time with the disciples.

26 From Attalia, Paul and Barnabas sailed back to Antioch of Syria, where they had been committed to the grace of God for the work they had now completed. The church at Antioch had sent them on the missionary adventure. The saints there had been praying for them. They understood their responsibility to missions. They would be glad to have them back with a lot of exciting news to share.

27 On arriving there, they gathered the church together and reported all that God had done through them and how He had opened a door of faith to the Gentiles. "A door of faith" is a metaphor corresponding to the idea of entering God's kingdom. The church was eager to hear about the exploits among the Gentiles. Paul and Barnabas kept their success or achievement in the proper perspective. "They saw themselves as instruments through which God had accomplished His purposes; and all the glory went to Him. That is an essential perspective for a servant of the Lord."[2]

28 With their mission accomplished, the missionaries were back ministering in their home church. They stayed there a long time with the disciples. Paul and Barnabas needed a complete rest and there was no better place to have that than in Antioch. Some scholars believe that Paul probably wrote his epistle to the Galatia while staying in Antioch.

NOTES

1. Derek W. H. Thomas, *Acts: Reformed Expository Commentary* (Phillipsburg, NJ: P&R Publishing Co., 2011), p. 391.
2. John MacArthur, *The MacArthur New Testament Commentary: Acts 13-28* (Chicago, IL: Moody Publishers, 1996), p. 57.

CHAPTER 7

THE JERUSALEM COUNCIL - PART 1

Acts 15:1-21

Strife on Ceremonial Law

Verses 1-5: Certain people came down from Judea to Antioch and were teaching the believers: "Unless you are circumcised, according to the custom taught by Moses, you cannot be saved." ² This brought Paul and Barnabas into sharp dispute and debate with them. So Paul and Barnabas were appointed, along with some other believers, to go up to Jerusalem to see the apostles and elders about this question. ³ The church sent them on their way, and as they traveled through Phoenicia and Samaria, they told how the Gentiles had been converted. This news made all the believers very glad. ⁴ When they came to Jerusalem, they were welcomed by the church and the apostles and elders, to whom they reported everything God had done through them. ⁵ Then some of the believers who belonged to the party of the Pharisees stood up and said, "The Gentiles must be circumcised and required to keep the law of Moses."

1 Chapter 15 should be regarded as the turning point in the book of Acts. It deals with the Jerusalem council of A.D. 49. "In this chapter Jerusalem is still the focus of interest, and Peter makes his final appearance in the story."[1]

Certain people came down from Judea to Antioch and were teaching the believers: "Unless you are circumcised, according to the custom taught by Moses, you cannot be saved." The inclusion of Gentiles into the church created some problems for the Jewish believers. These so-called

Judaizers had the opinion that Gentiles could not become Christians unless they were first circumcised. In other words, one must first become a Jew in order to become a Christian. In order to be saved, a Gentile must be circumcised and obey the law of Moses. The future of the church of Christ and its doctrine were at stake.

2 This brought Paul and Barnabas, the apostles to the Gentiles, into sharp dispute and debate with the Judaizers. So Paul and Barnabas were appointed, along with some other believers, to go up to Jerusalem to see the apostles and elders about this conflict. The difference of opinion caused great strife in the church. The vital issue could not be resolved at Antioch. They decided to bring the issue before the apostles in Jerusalem and obtain a ruling with apostolic authority. A delegation was sent to Jerusalem for the apostles and elders to settle the serious problem. The church at Jerusalem was still regarded as the mother church.

3 The church sent them on their way, and the delegation went along the coast and passed through Phoenicia. Then they went to Samaria, which had been evangelized by Philip. With no hotels along the way, they depended on the hospitality of the churches along their path. As they passed through these places, they told how the Gentiles had been converted. This news made all the believers very glad. Good news always cheers people up.

4 When they came to Jerusalem, they were welcomed by the church and the apostles and elders. They reported everything God had done through them, with them serving as His fellow laborers. They talked about the conversion of the Gentiles and the baptism with the Holy Spirit. They also included accounts of persecution as well as the signs and wonders. This was the third time Paul was visiting Jerusalem since his conversion.

5 Then some of the believers who belonged to the party of the Pharisees stood up and said, "The Gentiles must be circumcised and required to keep the law of Moses." Some of the Pharisaic believers insisted that the Gentiles must be circumcised and keep the law of Moses for them to be accepted in the body of Christ. In other words, they claimed that the prerequisite for the salvation of Gentile believers was circumcision.

Paul himself was raised a Pharisee and understood the narrow-minded intolerance of the Pharisees. This was somewhat a racial issue.

Peter's Address: Reviewing the Past

Verses 6-11: The apostles and elders met to consider this question. ⁷ After much discussion, Peter got up and addressed them: "Brothers, you know that some time ago God made a choice among you that the Gentiles might hear from my lips the message of the gospel and believe. ⁸ God, who knows the heart, showed that he accepted them by giving the Holy Spirit to them, just as he did to us. ⁹ He did not discriminate between us and them, for he purified their hearts by faith. ¹⁰ Now then, why do you try to test God by putting on the necks of Gentiles a yoke that neither we nor our ancestors have been able to bear? ¹¹ No! We believe it is through the grace of our Lord Jesus that we are saved, just as they are."

6 The potential divisive matter was not left to the congregation to decide. The apostles and elders, with maturity and the leading of the Spirit, met to consider this question. This could not be a trivial, minor decision. We are not told the details of how they arrived at the decision on the matter. They might have asked God to speak through prophecy or allow open discussion among themselves.

7 After much discussion, Peter got up and addressed them: "Brothers, you know that some time ago God made a choice among you that the Gentiles might hear from my lips the message of the gospel and believe." In his speech, Peter gave four proofs that God saves by grace. First, Peter reminded them how God used him to bring the message of salvation to Cornelius and his household without circumcision. It was God who took the initiative in saving the Gentiles.

8 Second, God, who knows the heart, showed that He accepted the Gentiles by giving the Holy Spirit to them, just as to Jews. Being an omniscient God, He knew that the hearts of the Gentiles were ready to receive His Spirit. He gave them the Spirit to confirm that they were truly born again. While men focus on outward appearance, God looks at the heart (1 Samuel 16:7). God's approval should make us accept them.

9 Third, God did not discriminate between the Jews and Gentiles, for He purified their hearts by faith. For centuries, God had made a distinction between Jews and Gentiles. Due to the work of Christ, the wall of partition separating the Jews and Gentiles has been removed. Since the work of Christ on Calvary, God does not differentiate between Jews and Gentiles. In pouring out the Holy Spirit, God does not make the slightest difference between Jews and Gentiles

10 Fourth, why do you try to test God by putting on the necks of Gentiles a yoke that neither we nor our ancestors have been able to bear? Peter warned the Judaizers not to test God. It would be unfair to ask the Gentiles to carry the yoke of the law which the Jews themselves could not bear. It was sheer folly to expect the Gentiles to follow what had not worked for the Jews. They must avoid having a double standard.

11 Peter concluded by saying, "No! We believe it is through the grace of our Lord Jesus that we are saved, just as they are." He answered the question in verse 10 as no. Whether for Jews or Gentiles, there is only one way of salvation—through the grace of the Lord Jesus Christ. All believers are God's people on the basis of grace. Grace is unmerited favor. It is getting what we don't deserve. This verse contains the last recorded words of Peter in the book of Acts.

James' Advice: Looking at the Future

*Verses 12-21: The whole assembly became silent as they listened to Barnabas and Paul telling about the signs and wonders God had done among the Gentiles through them. *[13]* When they finished, James spoke up. "Brothers," he said, "listen to me. *[14]* Simon has described to us how God first intervened to choose a people for his name from the Gentiles. *[15]* The words of the prophets are in agreement with this, as it is written:*

[16] *"'After this I will return*
    and rebuild David's fallen tent.
Its ruins I will rebuild,
    and I will restore it,
[17] *that the rest of mankind may seek the Lord,*
    even all the Gentiles who bear my name,

33

says the Lord, who does these things'—
¹⁸ things known from long ago.
¹⁹ "It is my judgment, therefore, that we should not make it difficult for the Gentiles who are turning to God. ²⁰ Instead we should write to them, telling them to abstain from food polluted by idols, from sexual immorality, from the meat of strangled animals and from blood. ²¹ For the law of Moses has been preached in every city from the earliest times and is read in the synagogues on every Sabbath."

12 Peter's argument was undisputable. His words quieted the congregation. The whole assembly became silent as they anxiously listened to Barnabas and Paul telling about the signs and wonders God had done among the Gentiles through them. Barnabas' name appears first because he was more known to the brethren at Jerusalem. The signs and wonders served as a confirmation that God was with them. They also served as irrefutable evidence that they were speaking on God's behalf. Paul and Barnabas reinforced what Peter said—God had granted full acceptance to the Gentiles. God accepted the Gentiles by faith through grace without circumcision.

13 When Paul and Barnabas had finished speaking, James spoke up. "Brothers," he said, "listen to me." James was the presiding elder in the Jerusalem church and his speech had real authority. He was highly respected. He was the half-brother of Jesus (Galatians 1:19). He did not know the Lord until after Jesus resurrected. Seeing his resurrected brother alive changed him. He wrote the epistle that bears his name. He was a legalist and was acceptable to the legalistic group in the Jerusalem church. The church tradition calls him by the nickname as "James the Just." The unofficial delegates in Antioch cited his name (Galatians 2:12).

14 Simon Peter had just described how God first intervened to choose a people for His name from the Gentiles. James was referring to Peter's visit to Cornelius. He discerned the fact that God called out people to form the body of Christ, the *ekklesia* (a church or assembly). God first called the Jews at Pentecost. He then used Peter to call out the Gentiles, starting at the house of Cornelius.

15-18 The words of the prophets are in agreement with this, as it is written: "After this I will return and rebuild David's fallen tent. Its ruins I will rebuild, and I will restore it, that the rest of mankind may seek the Lord, even all the Gentiles who bear my name, says the Lord, who does these things— things known from long ago."

The prophets agree concerning the fact that God is calling and choosing the Gentiles to be a part of His kingdom (e.g. Isaiah 42:6; Malachi 1:11). To support this, James appealed to Scripture and quoted Amos 9:11,12 from LXX, the Greek translation of the OT. The prophet describes future events. The quote speaks about the salvation and inclusion of the Gentiles, who are outside the covenant community of Israel.

This does not mean that God has forgotten His promises to Israel. He will restore the ruins of the kingdom of David and establish his rule over the nations. The prophecy awaits its fulfillment. God foreknew that the Jews would largely reject His Son and He used it to bring in the church. "God revealed these truths gradually to His people, but His plan had been settled from the beginning."[2]

19 James continued, "It is my judgment, therefore, that we should not make it difficult for the Gentiles who are turning to God." They should not ask the Gentiles to observe the rituals as requirements for salvation. God had set them free and they should not be troubled with religious scruples. The route the Judaizers were suggesting could be regarded as a yoke too heavy to be carried.

20 Instead, James recommended that the council should write them, telling them to abstain from four things. First, they should avoid food polluted by idols. Such food was offered to pagan idols and they should not eat it. Second, they should avoid sexual immorality. Christians are prohibited from engaging in fornication and are encouraged to be faithful to their marriage vows. "In all their marriage relations and conduct with the opposite sex, the Gentiles were to do nothing offensive to God's law or Jewish sensibilities."[3]

Third, the Gentiles should abstain from the meat of strangled animals. When an animal is killed by strangulation, some of its blood will remain and make it unfit for consumption. Fourth, they should avoid blood. Meat with blood was forbidden because life in the flesh is in the blood (Leviticus 17:10-13). These four restrictions were prescribed by James in order to please God and make fellowship easier and smooth between Jews and Gentiles. They would also serve to maintain the unity of the church.

21 For the law of Moses, which supports these four things to be avoided, has been preached in every city from the earliest times and is read in the synagogues on every Sabbath. Moses had plenty of preachers and was preached every Sabbath. If the Gentiles want to know more about the Jewish law, they have plenty of opportunity to do so in the local synagogues. James concluded his address by saying that while Moses was being preached weekly, they would preach the message of grace based on the work of Christ.

NOTES

1. John R. W. Stott, *The Message of Acts* (Downers Grove, IL: IVP Academic, 1990), p. 241.
2. Warren W. Wiersbe, *Be Daring: Acts 13-28* (Colorado Springs, CO: David C. Cook, 1988), p. 34.
3. John MacArthur, *The MacArthur New Testament Commentary: Acts 13-28* (Chicago, IL: Moody Publishers, 1996), p. 71.

CHAPTER 8

THE JERUSALEM COUNCIL - PART 2

Acts 15:22-41

The Council's Letter

Verses 22-29: *Then the apostles and elders, with the whole church, decided to choose some of their own men and send them to Antioch with Paul and Barnabas. They chose Judas (called Barsabbas) and Silas, men who were leaders among the believers.* ²³ *With them they sent the following letter:*

The apostles and elders, your brothers,

To the Gentile believers in Antioch, Syria and Cilicia:

Greetings.

²⁴ *We have heard that some went out from us without our authorization and disturbed you, troubling your minds by what they said.* ²⁵ *So we all agreed to choose some men and send them to you with our dear friends Barnabas and Paul—* ²⁶ *men who have risked their lives for the name of our Lord Jesus Christ.* ²⁷ *Therefore we are sending Judas and Silas to confirm by word of mouth what we are writing.* ²⁸ *It seemed good to the Holy Spirit and to us not to burden you with anything beyond the following requirements:* ²⁹ *You are to abstain from food sacrificed to idols, from blood, from the meat of strangled animals and from sexual immorality. You will do well to avoid these things.*

Farewell.

22 Then the apostles and elders, along with the whole Jerusalem church, decided to choose some of their own men and send them to Antioch with Paul and Barnabas. This was a wise decision. They chose Judas (called Barsabbas) and Silas (also known as Silvanus), men who were leaders among the believers. Judas was a Jew, while Silas was a Gentile. We know nothing about Judas, but we know that Silas would become an associate with Paul on his ministry. Both of them were prophets (v. 32). These four men would deliver the proceedings of the Jerusalem council to the church at Antioch.

23 With them they sent a letter. Although the four men would talk about the council's decision, the Jerusalem council put their decision in writing to avoid any misunderstanding. The front part of the letter consists of three elements. First, it shows that the letter is from the apostles, elders, and brothers of the Jerusalem church. The letter was possibly signed by them. By calling themselves "your brothers," they acknowledged that they were one with the Gentiles.

Second, it is addressed to the Gentile believers in Antioch, Syria and Cilicia. Antioch is named first because the original controversy started from there. "Syria and Cilicia were administered at this time as a single Roman district, of which Antioch was the capital."[1] Third, it begins with greetings. The word for greetings literally means "rejoice."

24 We have heard that some went out from us without our authorization and disturbed you, troubling your minds by what they said. The Judaizers were the troublemakers who had disturbed the Antioch church without any authorization from the church in Jerusalem. The council somehow disassociated itself from the false teachers or circumcision party, who pretended to be endorsed by the leaders of the church.

25,26 So we all agreed to choose some men and send them to you with our dear friends Barnabas and Paul—men who have risked their lives for the name of our Lord Jesus Christ. Paul and Barnabas were acknowledged as dear friends. The word about them was particularly warm, recognizing the legitimacy of their ministry to the Gentiles. They had literally risked their lives for believers. They were willing to suffer to the sake of Christ. They faced persecution and were nearly stoned to death.

27 Therefore we are sending Judas and Silas to confirm by word of mouth what we are writing. In the mouth of two or three witnesses, every word is established (Matthew 18:6). The two accredited messengers would give a verbal confirmation to the letter. They would tell how the decision was reached. Although letters are good means of putting things in writing, they are poor substitutes for oral communication.

28,29 It seemed good to the Holy Spirit and to us not to burden you with anything beyond the following requirements: You are to abstain from food sacrificed to idols, from blood, from the meat of strangled animals and from sexual immorality. You will do well to avoid these things. The items in verse 29 are taken from James' earlier address in verse 20, except for a change in wording and order.

The entire church at Jerusalem was careful to let the Holy Spirit lead them in making this important decision. We should be thankful that the council reached this decision because a lot was at stake. The Gentiles must avoid any involvement or association with idolatry. They must abstain from the meat of strangled animals. They must shun immorality. Avoiding these things would create a good atmosphere for fellowship between Jews and Gentiles. This is a loving compromise between the two groups. "If the Jews could give up their insistence on circumcision and on keeping the entire Mosaic law, the Gentiles could give up these things too."[2]

The Delivery of the Letter

Verses 30-35: So the men were sent off and went down to Antioch, where they gathered the church together and delivered the letter. [31] The people read it and were glad for its encouraging message. [32] Judas and Silas, who themselves were prophets, said much to encourage and strengthen the believers. [33] After spending some time there, they were sent off by the believers with the blessing of peace to return to those who had sent them. [34] [35] But Paul and Barnabas remained in Antioch, where they and many others taught and preached the word of the Lord.

30 So the men were sent off and went down to Antioch. They gathered the church together and delivered the letter from the church at Jerusalem. The letter was read in the presence of the entire church. "The whole church had been unsettled and anxiously awaiting the decision from the Jerusalem meeting and their response was one of joy and gladness."[3]

31 The people read it and were pleased and glad for its encouraging message. The message that salvation was through grace was a great consolation. Satan's attempt to introduce false teachings and divide the church along racial lines was frustrated. He loves to agitate us and fill us with fear and anxiety. But he is no match for the Holy Spirit who dwells in us and comforts us.

32 Judas and Silas, who themselves were recognized prophets, said much to encourage and strengthen the believers. They did more than just confirm the letter. They encouraged the people because the letter imposed some restrictions. Being prophets, the Holy Spirit might have used them to prophesy and encourage the church. We are not told what happened to the Judaizers. But we know that the letter from Jerusalem discredited and silenced them.

33 Judas and Silas were in no hurry to leave. After spending some time in Antioch, they were sent off by the believers with the blessing of peace and with prayers for their safety. The "blessing of peace" shows their favorable and warm response to the content of the letter. "It seems that they were dismissed in a formal way as they were received in a formal way."[4] Judas and Silas returned to the church in Jerusalem, to those who had sent them.

34 This verse is missing in some manuscripts. Some manuscripts add "but Silas decided to remain there." It seems that Judas went back to Jerusalem while Silas remained in Antioch. Others believe that Silas did go back to Jerusalem, but was later asked by Paul to come back to Antioch.

35 But Paul and Barnabas remained in Antioch, where they and many others taught and preached the Word of the Lord. As usual, Paul and Barnabas threw themselves into the work of Bible teaching and evangelizing. Like this missionary team, every believer should use his or her gifts to make known the Good News of salvation through Jesus Christ.

Disagreement between Paul and Barnabas

Verses 36-41: Some time later Paul said to Barnabas, "Let us go back and visit the believers in all the towns where we preached the word of the Lord and see how they are doing." ³⁷ Barnabas wanted to take John, also called Mark, with them, ³⁸ but Paul did not think it wise to take him, because he had deserted them in Pamphylia and had not continued with them in the work. ³⁹ They had such a sharp disagreement that they parted company. Barnabas took Mark and sailed for Cyprus, ⁴⁰ but Paul chose Silas and left, commended by the believers to the grace of the Lord. ⁴¹ He went through Syria and Cilicia, strengthening the churches.

36 This passage introduces us to the beginning of the second missionary journey of Paul. Some time later Paul said to Barnabas, "Let us go back and visit the believers in all the towns where we preached the word of the Lord and see how they are doing." It was not that Paul became bored pastoring the local church at Antioch. Having the gift of an evangelist, Paul felt passionate about saving the lost. He later wrote, "Woe to me if I do not preach the gospel" (1 Corinthians 9:16). He was also committed to revisiting those who were converted during the first missionary journey. He longed to see the converts again and help them grow spiritually.

37,38 Barnabas wanted to take John, also called Mark, with them but Paul did not think it wise to take him, because he had deserted them in Pamphylia and had not continued with them in the work. The two missionaries were at loggerheads. On one hand, Paul lost confidence in John Mark who deserted them before. On the other hand, Barnabas wanted to give his cousin Mark a second chance. The family tie between Barnabas and Mark complicated the situation. Barnabas was just as determined as Paul. The two strong-willed apostles clashed sharply.

39 They had such a sharp disagreement that they parted company. After the split, Barnabas took Mark and sailed for Cyprus, where he grew up (Acts 4:36). True to his name, as Son of Encouragement, Barnabas saw the great potential in the young man and helped to turn things around in his life. This is the last time Barnabas is mentioned in Acts. He quietly continued serving the Lord. Luke focuses exclusively on his hero, Paul.

40 But Paul chose Silas and left, commended by the believers to the grace of the Lord. They sought the blessing of the church before leaving. They headed north to the cities of southern Galatia. As we would see later, Silas proved to be a wise choice. Like Paul, Silas was a Roman citizen. He coauthored the Thessalonian epistles with Paul.

Thus, Paul and Barnabas went their separate ways. Although the disagreement resulted in separation, there were now two missionary teams, instead of one, and their impact had doubled. There are times when separation can be a legitimate option.

41 Paul with Silas went forth on Paul's second missionary journey. They went through Syria and Cilicia, strengthening the churches. Syria was the region in which Antioch was the capital, while Cilicia was the neighboring territory containing Tarsus, the home city of Paul. It would not be expedient for Saul to visit Cyprus as he did during his first missionary journey because Barnabas and Mark were already there.

NOTES

1. John MacArthur, *The MacArthur New Testament Commentary: Acts 13-28* (Chicago, IL: Moody Publishers, 1996), p. 72.
2. John Phillips, *Exploring Acts* (Grand Rapids, MI: Kregel Publications, 1986), p. 301.
3. Derek Carlsen, *Faith & Courage: Commentary on Acts* (Arlington Heights, IL: Christian Liberty Press, 2000), p. 360.
4. H. Leo Boles, H., *Acts* (Nashville, TN: Gospel Advocate Co., 1989), p. 246.

CHAPTER 9

PAUL IN MACEDONIA

Acts 16:1-15

Paul Returns to Derbe and Lystra

Verses 1-5: Paul came to Derbe and then to Lystra, where a disciple named Timothy lived, whose mother was Jewish and a believer but whose father was a Greek. ² The believers at Lystra and Iconium spoke well of him. ³ Paul wanted to take him along on the journey, so he circumcised him because of the Jews who lived in that area, for they all knew that his father was a Greek. ⁴ As they traveled from town to town, they delivered the decisions reached by the apostles and elders in Jerusalem for the people to obey. ⁵ So the churches were strengthened in the faith and grew daily in numbers.

1 Paul was taking a route different from the one he took on his first missionary journey. He came to Derbe and then to Lystra. He approached the region from the east on this occasion. This explains why the cities are named in reverse order from Acts 14:6. Paul with Barnabas had visited these cities during their first missionary journey (Acts 14:6). It was in Lystra that Paul healed a crippled man. At Lystra, a disciple named Timothy joined the missionary team. Timothy lived in Lystra with his family. His mother was Jewish and a believer but his father was a Greek.

2 The faith and training given by his mother and grandmother made Timothy what he was. They had trained him in the Scriptures from his childhood. The believers at Lystra and Iconium spoke well of Timothy. The distance between Lystra and Iconium was shorter than that between

Lystra and Derbe. This explains why Timothy was known in Lystra and Iconium. He seemed to be a young man above reproach and was well qualified for service.

3 Paul recognized his potential and wanted to take him along on the journey. Timothy would be a perfect replacement for Mark. However, Paul circumcised him because of the Jews who lived in that area, for they all knew that his father was a Greek. Some have criticized Paul for doing this. "Paul's circumcision of Timothy had nothing to do with salvation; he did it for expediency's sake, to avoid placing an unnecessary stumbling block in the way of Jewish evangelism."[1] Paul's strategy was to become all things to all men so that he might win some (1 Corinthians 9:19-23).

Timothy's mother Eunice and grandmother Lois (2 Timothy 1:5) permitted him to go him with Paul. He would be Paul's companion for the rest of Paul's life. Paul would later call him his son in the Lord (1 Timothy 1:2).

4 As they traveled from town to town, they delivered the decisions reached by the apostles and elders in Jerusalem for the people to obey. They shared the decisions of the Jerusalem council—that salvation was mainly by grace. The apostolic council was considered as binding on all churches outside Jerusalem.

5 The blessings of God remained on the work of Paul, Silas, and Timothy. As a result of their missionary activities, the churches were strengthened in the faith and grew daily in numbers. This is God's perfect will for His church—evangelistic and growing in number. It is His desire to bless His church and add to its number. We must evangelize sinners and edify saints.

The Call to Macedonia

Verses 6-10: Paul and his companions traveled throughout the region of Phrygia and Galatia, having been kept by the Holy Spirit from preaching the word in the province of Asia. [7] When they came to the border of Mysia, they tried to enter Bithynia, but the Spirit of Jesus would not allow them to. [8] So they passed by Mysia and went down to Troas. [9] During the night Paul had a vision of a man of Macedonia standing and begging him, "Come over to Macedonia and help us." [10] *After Paul had seen the vision, we got ready at once to leave for Macedonia, concluding that God had called us to preach the gospel to them.*

6 Paul and his companions traveled throughout the region of Phrygia and Galatia. It was the region westward from Iconium. They were forbidden by the Holy Spirit from preaching the Word in the province of Asia. The forbidding might have come through prophecy since both Paul and Silas were prophets. It was not yet time to evangelize Asia Minor. Paul could not go there. The temptation was to force open a door, but the Spirit says, "Wait."

7 The missionaries did not know where to go. When they came to the border of Mysia, the natural course of action would be to head north into the populated area of Bithynia, but the Spirit of Jesus would not allow them to. The Spirit of Jesus is another name for the Holy Spirit. The Holy Spirit was directing their movements—not Asia, not Bithynia, not now. He set the agenda and directed the travel itinerary. Paul was a prayer-saturated and Spirit-sensitized man. He must have been burdened as they passed city and city, forbidden to preach in them.

8 With no options left, they passed by Mysia and avoided it. They went down to Troas, the port city of the ancient Greece. It's proper name was Alexandria Troas. God's leading of His own is never without purpose. He brought Paul and his companions to Troas where He wanted them to be. Troas turned out to be a place of seeing a vision.

9 During the night Paul had a vision of a man of Macedonia standing and begging him, "Come over to Macedonia and help us." The missionary team was guided by the Holy Spirit directly speaking to them or through a vision. The Holy Spirit closes some doors in order to open other doors. This vision marks an important turning point in history because it resulted in the evangelization of Europe. In His providence, God led Paul and his companions west into Europe, not east into Asia Minor.

10 After Paul had seen the vision, he and his companions got ready at once to leave for Macedonia, concluding that God had called them to preach the gospel to the Macedonians. This would be the first time the gospel would enter Europe. This verse begins the "we" passages in Acts. It indicates that Luke was now part of the missionary team. Some have suggested that Luke was a Greek from Macedonia. He was a practicing physician at Troas.

Conversion in Philippi

Verses 11-15: From Troas we put out to sea and sailed straight for Samothrace, and the next day we went on to Neapolis. ¹² From there we traveled to Philippi, a Roman colony and the leading city of that district of Macedonia. And we stayed there several days. ¹³ On the Sabbath we went outside the city gate to the river, where we expected to find a place of prayer. We sat down and began to speak to the women who had gathered there. ¹⁴ One of those listening was a woman from the city of Thyatira named Lydia, a dealer in purple cloth. She was a worshiper of God. The Lord opened her heart to respond to Paul's message. ¹⁵ When she and the members of her household were baptized, she invited us to her home. "If you consider me a believer in the Lord," she said, "come and stay at my house." And she persuaded us.

11 The missionary team, consisting of Paul, Silas, Timothy, and Luke, were directed by the Spirit to go to Macedonia. From Troas they put out to sea and sailed straight for Samothrace, which was an island in the Aegean Sea. It is in an unmistakable location in between Troas and Neapolis. The next day they went on to Neapolis, which was the port city for Philippi. The distance from Troas to Neapolis was bout 150 miles. The missionary team did not stop at Samothrace and Neapolis to preach.

12 From Neapolis they traveled to Philippi, about ten miles inward. Philippi was a Roman colony and the leading city of that district of Macedonia. It received its name in 350 B.C. from King Philip II of Macedon, who was the father of Alexander the Great. The missionaries stayed there several days preaching the gospel. It was there that the gospel was first proclaimed on European soil. Today Philippi is a small village.

13 In Philippi, there were no Jewish synagogues for the missionary team to operate in. By the Jewish rule, it required the presence of ten male

Jews to form a synagogue. The city was essentially a military output of the Roman government and few Jews lived there. On the Sabbath the missionary team went outside the city gate to the Gangites River, where they expected to find a place of prayer. They sat down and began to speak to the women who had gathered there.

14 One of those listening and praying was a woman from the city of Thyatira named Lydia. The church at Thyatira was one the seven churches addressed by the Lord in the book of Revelation (Revelation 2:18-29). She was a dealer in purple cloth and a worshiper of God. The story of Jesus rang true to her. Her mind was prepared to hear Paul. The Lord opened her heart to respond to Paul's message. She became the first convert in Europe.

15 Paul regarded baptism as important, but not necessary for salvation. Baptism is the sign of the covenant in the NT. It denotes union with Christ. Lydia and the members of her household were baptized. This is the second household baptism in Acts. After the baptism, Lydia invited the missionaries to her home. She wanted to bless the missionaries by her hospitality. "If you consider me a believer in the Lord," she said, "come and stay at my house." She begged and persuaded them. Every Christian should be hospitable like Lydia.

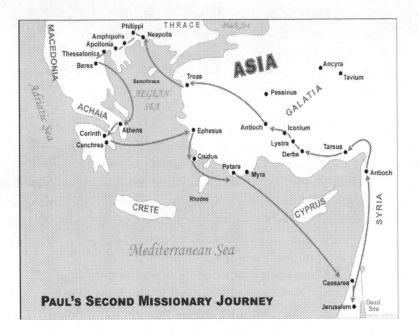

Source: www.biblestudy.org

NOTES

1. John MacArthur, *The MacArthur New Testament Commentary: Acts 13-28* (Chicago, IL: Moody Publishers, 1996), p. 84.

CHAPTER 10

PAUL AND SILAS IN PRISON

Acts 16:16-40

Paul Casts Out an Evil Spirit

Verses 16-21: Once when we were going to the place of prayer, we were met by a female slave who had a spirit by which she predicted the future. She earned a great deal of money for her owners by fortune-telling. [17] She followed Paul and the rest of us, shouting, "These men are servants of the Most High God, who are telling you the way to be saved." [18] She kept this up for many days. Finally Paul became so annoyed that he turned around and said to the spirit, "In the name of Jesus Christ I command you to come out of her!" At that moment the spirit left her. [19] When her owners realized that their hope of making money was gone, they seized Paul and Silas and dragged them into the marketplace to face the authorities. [20] They brought them before the magistrates and said, "These men are Jews, and are throwing our city into an uproar [21] by advocating customs unlawful for us Romans to accept or practice."

16 The missionaries might have been going to the place of prayer week after week for a period of time. Once when they were going to the place of prayer, they were met by a female slave who had a spirit by which she predicted the future. She was a medium working with evil spirits to make "inspired" speeches. She earned a great deal of money for her owners by fortune-telling. People would come to her in order for her to tell them things about their future and give them guidance. The girl was in double bondage: to evil spirits and to her masters.

17 On this particular day, she followed Paul and the rest of the missionary team, shouting, "These men are servants of the Most High God, who are telling you the way to be saved." What the demon-possessed girl was saying was true. Even the evil spirit recognized who Paul was. But Jesus never accepted the testimony of demons. Paul did not appreciate that testimony either.

18 She kept this up for many days. Finally Paul could not stand it any longer. He became so annoyed that he turned around and said to the spirit, "In the name of Jesus Christ I command you to come out of her!" At that moment the spirit left her. The spirit obeyed the apostolic authority of Paul. Casting out evil spirits is one of the signs that follow Jesus' believers (Mark 16:17).

19 When her owners realized that their hope of making money was gone, they seized Paul and Silas and dragged them into the marketplace to face the authorities or magistrates. The marketplace was where main activities took place. Instead of them rejoicing at the deliverance of their slave girl, they were mad at Paul for getting rid of their source of income. Paul's emancipation of the slave girl had put them out of business. This got Paul and Silas in trouble.

20,21 They brought the two missionaries (Paul and Silas) before the magistrates. Their accusers said, "These men are Jews, and are throwing our city into an uproar by advocating customs unlawful for us Romans to accept or practice." The accusation was serious enough to manipulate the crowd in the marketplace. The main problem was not that the missionaries had performed exorcism on the demon-possessed girl. It was rather on the basis that Paul and Silas were Jews causing an uproar. "Jews were not like other people. They did not worship the gods, they were clannish, and they would not buy meat in Gentile markets."[1]

Paul and Silas in Prison

Verses 22-28: The crowd joined in the attack against Paul and Silas, and the magistrates ordered them to be stripped and beaten with rods. [23] After they had been severely flogged, they were thrown into prison, and the jailer was commanded to guard them carefully. [24] When he received these orders, he put them in the inner cell and fastened their feet in the stocks.²⁵ About midnight Paul and Silas were praying and singing hymns to God, and the other prisoners were listening to them. ²⁶ Suddenly there was such a violent earthquake that the foundations of the prison were shaken. At once all the prison doors flew open, and everyone's chains came loose. ²⁷ The jailer woke up, and when he saw the prison doors open, he drew his sword and was about to kill himself because he thought the prisoners had escaped. ²⁸ But Paul shouted, "Don't harm yourself! We are all here!"

22 The crowd joined in the attack against Paul and Silas. False information is enough to excite a crowd. The magistrates ordered Paul and Silas to be stripped and beaten with rods. The excitement of the crowd was enough to convince the magistrates that the charges were correct. The magistrates did not investigate the charges against Paul and Silas or give them the chance to defend themselves. Instead, they ordered them to be flogged.

23 After they had been severely flogged, they were thrown into prison, and the jailer was commanded to guard them carefully. To make sure that they did not escape, Paul and Silas were placed in maximum security. One can imagine how discouraging Paul and Silas must have felt. Doing a good work landed them in prison.

24 When the jailer received these orders from the magistrates, he put Paul and Silas in the inner cell and fastened their feet in the stocks. Taking no chances, the jailer put them in the most secure part of the prison—the innermost cell, which was dark, dirty, and cold. This was the place reserved for dangerous criminals. Their feet were secured in the stocks which clamped the feet in an uncomfortable position.

25 The persecution did not intimidate Paul and Silas. About midnight Paul and Silas were worshiping the Lord. They were praying and singing hymns to God, and the other prisoners were listening to them. In spite of what they were going through physically, they maintained a joyful attitude. A believer can rejoice always (Philippians 4:4) because he or she knows that God causes all things to work together for good for those who love God (Romans 8:28).

26 God inhabits the praises of His people (Psalm 22:3, KJV). As Paul and Silas were praising God, God intervened by sending an earthquake. Suddenly there was such a violent earthquake that the foundations of the prison were shaken. At once all the prison doors flew open, and everyone's chains came loose. The earthquake woke up every prisoner and the jailer.

27 The jailer woke up, and when he saw the prison doors open, he drew his sword and was about to kill himself because he thought the prisoners had escaped. He knew that allowing the prisoners to escape would lead to his own death. He was liable to suffer the same punishment that the prisoners should have suffered. He wanted to avoid the disgrace of a far worse death than suicide.

28 Before the jailer killed himself, Paul shouted, "Don't harm yourself! We are all here!" None of the prisoners had left the prison. Why did the prisoners not run away? The earthquake was a supernatural work of God, who prevented the prisoners from escaping. Paul was kind and merciful to the jailer. He prevented the jailer from committing suicide.

The Conversion of the Jailer

Verses 29-34: *The jailer called for lights, rushed in and fell trembling before Paul and Silas. [30] He then brought them out and asked, "Sirs, what must I do to be saved?" [31] They replied, "Believe in the Lord Jesus, and you will be saved—you and your household." [32] Then they spoke the word of the Lord to him and to all the others in his house. [33] At that hour of the night the jailer took them and washed their wounds; then immediately he and all his household were baptized. [34] The jailer brought them into his house and set a meal before them; he was filled with joy because he had come to believe in God—he and his whole household.*

29 The jailer called for lights since it was dark, and rushed into the cells. He made a hasty investigation and found that no one had escaped, just as Paul said. He was overcome with fear and relief. He fell trembling before Paul and Silas. The jailer fell down before his prisoners. He saw the earthquake as a confirmation that Paul and Silas were God's spokesmen.

30 After bringing the missionaries out of their cell, the jailer wanted the salvation that Paul and Silas offered. He brought them out and asked, "Sirs, what must I do to be saved?" (This is an important question everyone should ask.) The question indicated a deep longing in his heart to get right with God. He was desperately in need for forgiveness and salvation.

31 They replied, "Believe in the Lord Jesus, and you will be saved—you and your household." No one comes to the Father except through Jesus (John 14:6). There is no other name by which we can be saved (Acts 4:12). When we believe in the Lord Jesus in our heart that God raised Him from the dead, we will be saved (Romans 10:9). Believing in Jesus is necessary for us to be saved and that means we trust Jesus for what He claims to be.

32 The Philippian jailer took Paul and Silas to his house. Then they spoke the Word of the Lord to him and to all the others in his house. They shared with them the message of the gospel. All his family members and servants heard the message of salvation that night. The jailer's household was composed of those who could understand the gospel. The entire family partook of these wonderful words of life.

33 At that hour of the night the jailer took Paul and Silas and washed their wounds. "It is touching to see the change in the attitude of the jailer as he washed the wounds of these two prisoners who are now his brothers in Christ."[2] Immediately he and all his household were baptized. By that act, they identified themselves with Christ. It shows that their salvation was genuine.

34 The jailer brought them into his house and set a meal before them. He showed hospitality to the two missionaries. A short while ago, he was planning to commit suicide. Now he was filled with joy because he had come to believe in God—he and his whole household. There is no greater joy than knowing our sins are forgiven. He had come to know a life superior to anything he had known.

Paul Declares His Roman Citizenship

Verses 35-40: When it was daylight, the magistrates sent their officers to the jailer with the order: "Release those men." ³⁶ The jailer told Paul, "The magistrates have ordered that you and Silas be released. Now you can leave. Go in peace." ³⁷ But Paul said to the officers: "They beat us publicly without a trial, even though we are Roman citizens, and threw us into prison. And now do they want to get rid of us quietly? No! Let them come themselves and escort us out." ³⁸ The officers reported this to the magistrates, and when they heard that Paul and Silas were Roman citizens, they were alarmed. ³⁹ They came to appease them and escorted them from the prison, requesting them to leave the city. ⁴⁰ After Paul and Silas came out of the prison, they went to Lydia's house, where they met with the brothers and sisters and encouraged them. Then they left.

35 When it was daylight, the magistrates sent their officers to the jailer with the order: "Release those men." That sounded like a good news. Why did the authorities decide to free Paul and Silas? Perhaps they knew that they had no legitimate case against the missionaries. They thought that the two Jewish troublemakers must have learned their lesson.

36 The jailer joyfully received the message. He told Paul, "The magistrates have ordered that you and Silas be released. Now you can leave. Go in peace." Paul and Silas were now free to go. They should leave the city peacefully without stirring up any more trouble. Paul, however, did not obey the orders of the jailer. He was not prepared to slip away quietly.

37 But Paul said to the officers: "They beat us publicly without a trial, even though we are Roman citizens, and threw us into prison. And now do they want to get rid of us quietly? No! Let them come themselves and escort us out." Paul and Silas could not depart quietly because it would set a bad precedent for the treatment of other missionaries. They intended to teach the unjust magistrates their lesson; they would think twice before abusing their authority again. They also wanted to leave a good witness for the new church in Philippi.

38 The officers reported this to the magistrates. When they heard that Paul and Silas were Roman citizens, they were alarmed. They realized that they had violated Roman law. "The magistrates were in an awkward position. On the one hand, they had no legal grounds for expelling two Roman citizens who were guilty of no crime. On the other hand, Paul and Silas's continued presence in Philippi could have provoked further violence."[3]

39 They came to appease them and escorted them from the prison, requesting them to leave the city. They showed Paul and Silas the respect due to Roman citizens. They were not commanding the missionaries but seeking their favor. Although they were asked to leave, they did so on their own terms. They must first say farewell to their friends.

40 After Paul and Silas came out of the prison, they went to Lydia's house, where they met with the brothers and sisters and encouraged them. It was to these Christians that Paul later wrote the Philippian epistle. Then they left and took the gospel message to the next city. Because Luke was not a Jew, he was not under pressure to leave. So he remained in Philippi. "Note that Luke returned to the third person 'they' in this verse, as the first 'we' section of Acts ends. This may indicate that Luke stayed behind in Philippi to continue the work while Paul and Silas moved on toward Athens. The next 'we' section begins at 20:5."[4]

NOTES

1. John Phillips, *Exploring Acts* (Grand Rapids, MI: Kregel Publications, 1986), p. 327.
2. Warren W. Wiersbe, *Be Daring: Acts 13-28* (Colorado Springs, CO: David C. Cook, 1988), p. 49.
3. John MacArthur, *The MacArthur New Testament Commentary: Acts 13-28* (Chicago, IL: Moody Publishers, 1996), p. 111.
4. B. Bruce Barton et al., *Life Application Bible Commentary: Acts* (Carol Stream, IL: Tyndale House Publishers, 1999), p. 290.

CHAPTER 11

IN THESSALONICA AND BEREA

Acts 17:1-15

Paul at Thessalonica

Verses 1-4: When Paul and his companions had passed through Amphipolis and Apollonia, they came to Thessalonica, where there was a Jewish synagogue. ² As was his custom, Paul went into the synagogue, and on three Sabbath days he reasoned with them from the Scriptures, ³ explaining and proving that the Messiah had to suffer and rise from the dead. "This Jesus I am proclaiming to you is the Messiah," he said. ⁴ Some of the Jews were persuaded and joined Paul and Silas, as did a large number of God-fearing Greeks and quite a few prominent women.

1 After leaving Philippi, Paul and his companions traveled southwest. When they had passed through Amphipolis and Apollonia, they came to Thessalonica, where there was a Jewish synagogue. This distance from Philippi to Thessalonica (today's Saloniki) was about 100 miles along the Egnatian Way, and it was a three-day journey.

They did not stop to preach the gospel at Amphipolis and Apollonia possibly because there were no Jewish synagogues there. Paul's evangelistic strategy was to evangelize big cities of the empire and leave the evangelization of rural areas to the residents of the big cities. Being the capital of Macedonia and center of commerce, Thessalonica was strategically located for the work of the Lord.

2 Paul was a Jew and he had access to the Jewish synagogue. As was his custom, Paul went into the synagogue, where he would find those who had a working knowledge of the OT Scripture. He would labor as a tentmaker during the week and then minister in the synagogue on the Sabbath. On three Sabbath days he reasoned with the Thessalonian Jews from the OT Scriptures. Paul loved his fellow Jews and wanted them to be saved (Romans 9:1-3). He boldly confronted them and supported himself with the Scriptures.

3 He explained and proved that the Messiah had to suffer and rise from the dead. It was difficult for the Jews to accept the Messiah's suffering, death, and resurrection. "This Jesus I am proclaiming to you is the Messiah," Paul said. The apostle carefully set one OT proof after another before them that Jesus of Nazareth is the Christ. As the next verse shows, Paul's reasoning with them was effective and productive.

4 Some of the Jews were persuaded and joined Paul and Silas, as did a large number of God-fearing Greeks and quite a few prominent women. Paul's powerful exposition coupled with the presence of the Holy Spirit led many to believe: (1) Jews; (2) God-fearing Greeks, and (3) prominent women. Among the converts were Aristarchus and Secundus who later became traveling companions with Paul (Acts 20:4). Paul would later write two epistles (1 & 2 Thessalonians) to believers in Thessalonica.

Jews Oppose the Missionaries

Verses 5-9: But other Jews were jealous; so they rounded up some bad characters from the marketplace, formed a mob and started a riot in the city. They rushed to Jason's house in search of Paul and Silas in order to bring them out to the crowd. ⁶ But when they did not find them, they dragged Jason and some other believers before the city officials, shouting: "These men who have caused trouble all over the world have now come here, ⁷ and Jason has welcomed them into his house. They are all defying Caesar's decrees, saying that there is another king, one called Jesus." ⁸ When they heard this, the crowd and the city officials were thrown into turmoil. ⁹ Then they made Jason and the others post bond and let them go.

5 But other Jews in the area were jealous of the success of Paul and Silas' ministry. They saw how fellow Jews and Gentiles embraced the gospel and turned to Christ. They resented the popularity of Paul and Silas and were moved with envy. So they rounded up some bad characters from the marketplace, formed a mob and started a riot in the city. They rushed to Jason's house in search of Paul and Silas in order to bring them out to the crowd. Jason was possibly one of Paul's converts and his home served as a base of operation for the new church. The plan of the mob misfired since the missionaries were not found in Jason's house.

6,7 But when they did not find them, the mob dragged Jason and some other believers with him before the city officials, shouting: "These men who have caused trouble all over the world have now come here, and Jason has welcomed them into his house. They are all defying Caesar's decrees, saying that there is another king, one called Jesus." The Jews made two charges against the missionaries. First, they accused them of causing trouble. They turned the place upside down. Second, they charged them with defying Caesar, claiming there was another king besides Caesar. And Jason was considered guilty by association.

8 When they heard the manipulative charges brought against the missionaries, the crowd and the city officials were thrown into turmoil. The people were greatly disturbed; they did not want to incur any trouble from Rome. The charges were serious and had to be taken as such. But they could not substantiate the charges.

9 Because Jason and other believers were innocent, they released them. They made Jason and the others post bond and let them go. In other words, they took security (a pledge or bail) from Jason and others before releasing them. Jason pledged his word not to harbor Paul in his house and Paul honored it. Paul might not be able to go back to Thessalonica, but he could write them some letters.

Paul in Berea

Verses 10-12: As soon as it was night, the believers sent Paul and Silas away to Berea. On arriving there, they went to the Jewish synagogue. ¹¹ Now the Berean Jews were of more noble character than those in Thessalonica, for they *received the message with great eagerness and examined the Scriptures every day to see if what Paul said was true. [12] As a result, many of them believed, as did also a number of prominent Greek women and many Greek men.*

10 As soon as it was night, the believers sent Paul and Silas away to Berea, which was about 60 miles away. They took them out of the city by night to avoid another public disturbance. On arriving in Berea, they went to the Jewish synagogue there. As usual, Paul went to the synagogue to share the same message that he preached in Thessalonica—the Messiah must suffer, die, and be raised from the dead.

11 Now the Berean Jews were of more noble character than those in Thessalonica, for they received the message with great eagerness and examined the Scriptures every day to see if what Paul said was true. They were open and receptive to God's truth. They were diligent in comparing Scripture with Scripture to see if Paul was teaching the truth. They saw the Scriptures as the sole authority for faith and practice.

12 As a result, many of them believed, as did also a number of prominent Greek women and many Greek men. In Thessalonica some of the Jews believed the gospel, while others let their old prejudices guide them. In Berea, however, many Jews believed and there was no opposition. Paul's witness and diligent Bible teaching led many to believe. A new church was born in Berea. The reputation of this church started to spread throughout the region and reached Thessalonica. But Paul's pleasant experience with the Bereans was short-lived.

Jews from Thessalonica Pursue Paul

Verses 13-15: But when the Jews in Thessalonica learned that Paul was preaching the word of God at Berea, some of them went there too, agitating the crowds and stirring them up. [14] The believers immediately sent Paul to the coast, but Silas and Timothy stayed at Berea. [15] Those who escorted Paul brought him to Athens and then left with instructions for Silas and Timothy to join him as soon as possible.

13 But when the Jews in Thessalonica learned that Paul was preaching the Word of God in Berea, some of them went there too, agitating the crowds and stirring them up. They were determined to prevent the gospel message from being preached anywhere. This shows how the Jews deeply hated the gospel and the missionaries. Satan used them to oppose the work of God.

14 The believers immediately sent Paul to the coast, but Silas and Timothy stayed in Berea to continue the work. Believers were concerned about Paul's safety. The hatred of the Jews was directed against Paul rather than against Silas and Timothy. As Chuck Smith said, "Paul has had a pretty rough ministry in Europe. In Philippi he was beaten and jailed. He escaped from there to Thessalonica, only to leave under the cover of darkness. And in Berea he is hurried out of town and placed on a ship to Athens."[1]

15 Those who escorted Paul brought him to Athens possibly by sea, a journey of more than 300 miles. They left with instructions for Silas and Timothy to join him as soon as possible. Paul would feel lonely in this city of the ancient world. He needed Silas and Timothy to be with him at their earliest opportunity. In 1Thessalonians 3:1-2, Paul indicates that Timothy came to Athens and was then sent to Thessalonica.

NOTES

1. Chuck Smith, *The Book of Acts* (Costa Mesa, CA: The Word for Today, 2013), p. 277.

CHAPTER 12

PAUL IN ATHENS

Acts 17:16-34

Paul Encounters the Philosophers

Verses 16-21: While Paul was waiting for them in Athens, he was greatly distressed to see that the city was full of idols. ¹⁷ So he reasoned in the synagogue with both Jews and God-fearing Greeks, as well as in the marketplace day by day with those who happened to be there. ¹⁸ A group of Epicurean and Stoic philosophers began to debate with him. Some of them asked, "What is this babbler trying to say?" Others remarked, "He seems to be advocating foreign gods." They said this because Paul was preaching the good news about Jesus and the resurrection. ¹⁹ Then they took him and brought him to a meeting of the Areopagus, where they said to him, "May we know what this new teaching is that you are presenting? ²⁰You are bringing some strange ideas to our ears, and we would like to know what they mean." ²¹ (All the Athenians and the foreigners who lived there spent their time doing nothing but talking about and listening to the latest ideas.)

16 Athens was the home of world famous philosophers—Socrates, Plato, Aristotle, etc. It used to be the intellectual center of the ancient world. It was also a cosmopolitan city of idols. Their culture had caused them to defy practically everything. While Paul was waiting for Timothy and Silas in Athens, he was greatly distressed to see that the city was full of idols—graven images made by foolish men (Psalm 115:4-8). Paul's spirit was being provoked as he looked at the idols. He knew that the people who consecrated their lives became as vile as the things they loved (Hosea 9:10b).

17 Godly anger should always lead to positive action. So Paul reasoned in the synagogue with both Jews and God-fearing Greeks, as well as in the marketplace day by day with those who happened to be there. His strategy was to meet his countrymen in the synagogue on the Sabbath. The rest of the week, he reasoned with the people who happened to be in the marketplace.

18 There were three major schools of philosophy in Athens—the Cynics, the Epicureans, and the Stoics. A group of Epicurean and Stoic philosophers began to debate with him. The Epicurean philosophy teaches that the pursuit of pleasure is the chief end of man. They took their name from Epicurus (341-270 B.C.) and were materialistic. The Stoic philosophy teaches that self-mastery is the greatest virtue and all of life is determined by the gods.

Referring to Paul, some of them asked, "What is this babbler trying to say?" Others remarked, "He seems to be advocating foreign gods." The intellectuals at Athens sneered at the gospel. They said this because Paul was preaching the good news about Jesus and the resurrection.

19,20 Then they took Paul and brought him to a meeting of the Areopagus, where they said to him, "May we know what this new teaching is that you are presenting? You are bringing some strange ideas to our ears, and we would like to know what they mean." The Areopagus bears the name Mars' Hill. It used to be a place where the noblest blood of Athens assembled. It was also the place where Socrates was arraigned and condemned. They invited Paul to the forum of Mars' Hill. They provided him a forum for Paul to formally express himself. They wanted to hear from him about the new teaching.

21 All the Athenians and the foreigners who lived there spent their time doing nothing but talking about and listening to the latest ideas. The Greeks prided themselves in welcoming novel ideas. This indicates why they were anxious to hear Paul's message.

Paul's Sermon on the Mars' Hill

Verses 22-31: Paul then stood up in the meeting of the Areopagus and said: "People of Athens! I see that in every way you are very religious. 23 For as I walked around and looked carefully at your objects of worship, I even found an altar with this inscription: TO AN UNKNOWN GOD. *So you are ignorant of the very thing you worship—and this is what I am going to proclaim to you. 24 "The God who made the world and everything in it is the Lord of heaven and earth and does not live in temples built by human hands. 25 And he is not served by human hands, as if he needed anything. Rather, he himself gives everyone life and breath and everything else. 26 From one man he made all the nations, that they should inhabit the whole earth; and he marked out their appointed times in history and the boundaries of their lands. 27 God did this so that they would seek him and perhaps reach out for him and find him, though he is not far from any one of us. 28 'For in him we live and move and have our being.' As some of your own poets have said, 'We are his offspring.' 29 "Therefore since we are God's offspring, we should not think that the divine being is like gold or silver or stone—an image made by human design and skill. 30 In the past God overlooked such ignorance, but now he commands all people everywhere to repent. 31 For he has set a day when he will judge the world with justice by the man he has appointed. He has given proof of this to everyone by raising him from the dead."*

22 Paul then stood up in the meeting of the Areopagus and said: "People of Athens! I see that in every way you are very religious." "Areopagus" refers to the hill of Mars, where the temple of Mars was located. The fact that the people were religious could be observed in every street in Athens. Religion is man's attempt to reach God, while Christianity is God's attempt to reach man. Paul began his speech by acknowledging the fact that the people of Athens were religious. He told us how he came to that conclusion in the next verse.

23 For as I walked around and looked carefully at your objects of worship, I even found an altar with this inscription:

63

TO AN UNKNOWN GOD

So you are ignorant of the very thing you worship—and this is what I am going to proclaim to you. They were so religious that they reserved an altar to "an unknown God," just in case a deity was missing. They knew about everything knowable, but they knew nothing about God. Paul was going to talk to them about the unknown God.

24 Paul started by stating that the true God made the world and everything in it; He is the Lord of heaven and earth. David wrote that "the earth is the LORD's and everything in it, the world, and all who live in it"(Psalm 24:1). The world and its orderliness did not come about by accident, but by a personal God. God does not live in temples built by human hands (1 Kings 8:27). Paul dismissed their idols as worthless (Psalm 115:4-8).

25 And God is not served by human hands, as if He needed anything. It is absurd to think that God would need our service (Psalm 50:9-12). Rather, He Himself gives everyone life and breath and everything else. He is the source of everything (James 1:17). "For from him and through him and to him are all things" (Romans 11:36). God is self-sufficient in and by Himself.

26 From one man He made all the nations, that they should inhabit the whole earth. All nations and races have a common origin in God. He marked out their appointed times in history and the boundaries of their lands. God not only created the whole world, but He also controls the destines of individuals and nations. The rise and fall of nations is under the control of the Almighty God. That they were living in Athens was by God's design, not a result of some cosmic accident. Having been created by God, He also desired a personal relationship with them.

27 The reason God ordered things like that is because we would seek him and perhaps reach out for Him and find Him, though he is not far from any one of us. There is within every man the deep desire for a meaningful relationship with the Creator. Man is incomplete without God. Nothing else but God will satisfy our souls. The God of creation is not far from us.

28 To buttress his point, Paul quoted two lines of Greek poetry. First, the poet Epimedes of Crete said, "For in him we live and move and have our being." The three verbs live, move, and being encompass the totally of human life. They show that we totally depend on God at every turn. Second, Aratus of Cilicia said, "We are his offspring." (Paul knew his literature well.) The Greeks could not claim ignorance because their poets acknowledge God's revelation in nature. This confirms the fact that all men are God's offspring, descending from Adam. We are all made in the image of God.

29 Therefore since we are God's offspring, it is silly to think that the divine being is like gold or silver or stone—an image made by human design and skill. God is Spirit (John 4:24) and cannot be represented by an image. The listed materials—gold, silver, and stone—may offer beauty, yet they cannot adequately express the reality of the divine. "If God created man, He must be more than a mere man-made idol. Paul used quotes from their own poets to highlight to his audience the absurdity of idolatry."[1]

30 In the past God deliberately overlooked or winked at such ignorance, but now He commands all people everywhere to repent. The Athenians' religious achievements were nothing but ignorant guesses in the darkness. Their way of worshipping God was perverse. The time for such forbearance was now past. God now demanded repentance from their idolatry and spiritual wickedness.

31 For God has set a day when He will judge the world with justice by the man He has appointed. The Father has committed all judgment to His Son, Jesus Christ (John 5:22-27). He has given proof of this to everyone by raising Him from the dead. Greek theology had no concept for the coming judgment or resurrection. Christ will come and judge the world in righteousness. As Derek Carlsen said, "The standard of judgment is known—God's righteousness. The day of judgment has been ordained in God's secret counsel and is inescapable. The Person who will do the actual judgment has been ordained by God. All of these are fixed and unmovable."[2]

Little Results in Athens

Verses 32-34: When they heard about the resurrection of the dead, some of them sneered, but others said, "We want to hear you again on this subject." ³³ At that, Paul left the Council. ³⁴ Some of the people became followers of Paul and believed. Among them was Dionysius, a member of the Areopagus, also a woman named Damaris, and a number of others.

32 Paul's preaching had three basic responses from the hearers—mockery, procrastination, and belief. When they heard about the resurrection of the dead, some of them sneered. They had no idea of a bodily resurrection Paul was talking about. Some would have regarded the idea of resurrection as a lunatic's imagination. They mocked Paul. But others said, "We want to hear you again on this subject." They never did hear Paul again. Procrastination is a dangerous game.

33 With the outburst of scoffing, Paul left the Council of the Areopagus. That outburst concluded his discussion with them. There was still some interest among the audience and some were converted. There is no mention in the NT of any church in this city. But it is clear that Paul left a body of believers behind. Paul left Athens, never to return there. He soon moved on to Corinth.

34 "Paul's preaching at Athens produced little result.... The gospel does not make its greatest impact among those who are wise after the flesh."[3] Paul's effort was not entirely fruitless. Some of the people there became followers of Paul and believed. Among them was Dionysius, a member of the Areopagus, also a woman named Damaris, and a number of others. "The Areopagites were a special group of select men who were considered to be the intellectual giants of the day—the aristocratic philosophers of Athens. Dionysius was one of these men."[4]

NOTES

1. John MacArthur, *The MacArthur New Testament Commentary: Acts 13-28* (Chicago, IL: Moody Publishers, 1996), p. 141.

2. Derek Carlsen, *Faith & Courage: Commentary on Acts* (Arlington Heights, IL: Christian Liberty Press, 2000), pp. 409,410.
3. John Phillips, *Exploring Acts* (Grand Rapids, MI: Kregel Publications, 1986), p. 355.
4. Chuck Smith, *The Book of Acts* (Costa Mesa, CA: The Word for Today, 2013), p. 286.

CHAPTER 13

PAUL IN CORINTH

Acts 18:1-17

The Companionship of Friends

Verses 1-4: After this, Paul left Athens and went to Corinth. ² There he met a Jew named Aquila, a native of Pontus, who had recently come from Italy with his wife Priscilla, because Claudius had ordered all Jews to leave Rome. Paul went to see them, ³ and because he was a tentmaker as they were, he stayed and worked with them. ⁴ Every Sabbath he reasoned in the synagogue, trying to persuade Jews and Greeks.

1 After this, Paul left Athens and went to Corinth, about a 50 mile journey. Corinth was a cosmopolitan and commercial center in Greece. It was on an isthmus, a narrow strip of land connecting two seas—the Ionian and the Aegean. Back then it was the political capital of Greece. "Corinth was the Vanity Fair of the Roman Empire, famous for the licentious worship of Venus."[1] The city was known for its great moral perversity. Money and vice came to Corinth and found a place there.

2 There in Corinth Paul met a Jew named Aquila, a native of Pontus, who had recently come from Italy with his wife Priscilla, because Claudius had ordered all Jews to leave Rome. The Jewish couple was forced to move their business from Italy to Corinth. Priscilla is mentioned first four out of the six times the couple were mentioned in the NT; some have speculated that she was more prominent than her husband. Paul went to see them. Having left Silas and Timothy in Macedonia, Paul probably needed the company of other believers like Aquila and Priscilla.

3 Because Paul was a tentmaker (or worker of leather) as they were, he stayed and worked with them. Paul probably learned this skill from his father. Even rabbis back then were supposed to support themselves through gainful employment and accept no compensation for their teaching. Paul naturally gravitated toward people of the same occupation and faith.

4 Paul chose to work and support himself in Corinth. While working with the Jewish couple during the week, every Sabbath Paul reasoned in the synagogue, trying to persuade Jews and Greeks to accept Jesus as the Messiah. As fellow believers, the couple accompanied Paul to the synagogue every Sabbath. This was Paul's predictable rule; he shared the gospel with the Jews first and then to the Gentiles.

Paul's Ministry at Corinth

Verses 5-11: When Silas and Timothy came from Macedonia, Paul devoted himself exclusively to preaching, testifying to the Jews that Jesus was the Messiah. ⁶ But when they opposed Paul and became abusive, he shook out his clothes in protest and said to them, "Your blood be on your own heads! I am innocent of it. From now on I will go to the Gentiles." ⁷ Then Paul left the synagogue and went next door to the house of Titius Justus, a worshiper of God. ⁸ Crispus, the synagogue leader, and his entire household believed in the Lord; and many of the Corinthians who heard Paul believed and were baptized. ⁹ One night the Lord spoke to Paul in a vision: "Do not be afraid; keep on speaking, do not be silent. ¹⁰ For I am with you, and no one is going to attack and harm you, because I have many people in this city." ¹¹ So Paul stayed in Corinth for a year and a half, teaching them the word of God.

5 When Silas and Timothy came from Macedonia, Paul devoted himself exclusively to preaching, testifying to the Jews that Jesus was the Messiah. The generous gift brought by Silas and Timothy from the brethren in Phillippi (Philippians 4:15) allowed him to devote himself fully to his missionary work. The arrival of Silas and Timothy brought encouragement to Paul and they also brought word about the perseverance of the saints in Thessalonica (1 Thessalonians 3:6-8).

6 Wherever Paul went, the Jews caused trouble against him. In Corinth, when they opposed Paul and became abusive, he shook out his clothes in protest and said to them, "Your blood be on your own heads! I am innocent of it. From now on I will go to the Gentiles." To have blood on your head means that you bear the responsibility of another person's death by not warning him (Ezekiel 317-21). Paul's decisive action symbolized his rejection of the Jews. He absolved himself from any responsibility connected with their fate. He resolved after this to focus his ministry to the Gentiles. This does not mean he would not attempt converting his fellow Jews or he would cease going to the synagogue first.

7 Then Paul left the synagogue and did not have to go far to find a convenient location. There was one next door, the house of Titius Justus, a worshiper of God. Titius might be one of the Corinthians that Paul converted as he was obviously sympathetic to the ministry of Paul. His house became the base of operations for Paul. However, by preaching so close to the synagogue, Paul angered the Jewish leadership.

8 Crispus, the synagogue leader, and his entire household believed in the Lord. As the synagogue leader, Crispus was responsible for regulating services, appointing those who would read the law, and selecting those who would preach. It seems that he lost his position in the synagogue due to his conversion to Christianity because a man named Sosthenes was later called the synagogue ruler (v. 17). Like Crispus, giving your life to Christ will always cost you something. Many of the Corinthians who heard Paul believed and were baptized.

9,10 The God of all comfort did not leave Paul alone in his downtrodden condition. One night the Lord spoke to Paul in a vision: "Do not be afraid; keep on speaking, do not be silent. For I am with you, and no one is going to attack and harm you, because I have many people in this city." This is one of the six visions received by Paul which were recorded in Acts.

In this particular vision, the Lord told Paul five things. First, Paul should not be afraid. Second, he should not be silent but he should keep speaking boldly. Third, the Lord promised to be with Paul (Isaiah 43:5). God's presence can dispel our fears. Fourth, the Lord assured him that no one would attack and harm Paul. Divine protection is the best one can hope for. Fifth, Corinth was an important city and God had many people there. Paul would not be prevented from completing his missionary work in Corinth.

11 With the encouragement from the Lord, Paul stayed in Corinth for a year and a half, teaching the church there the Word of God. For the next eighteen months, Paul was involved in the evangelization of the great city. He stayed there long enough to engage the surrounding areas. Because of Paul's ministry there, the church at Corinth became one of the largest of the early churches. It was possibly during this period that he wrote the two epistles to the Thessalonians.

The Frustration of His Enemies

Verses 12-17: While Gallio was proconsul of Achaia, the Jews of Corinth made a united attack on Paul and brought him to the place of judgment. ¹³ "This man," they charged, "is persuading the people to worship God in ways contrary to the law." ¹⁴ Just as Paul was about to speak, Gallio said to them, "If you Jews were making a complaint about some misdemeanor or serious crime, it would be reasonable for me to listen to you. ¹⁵ But since it involves questions about words and names and your own law—settle the matter yourselves. I will not be a judge of such things." ¹⁶ So he drove them off. ¹⁷ Then the crowd there turned on Sosthenes the synagogue leader and beat him in front of the proconsul; and Gallio showed no concern whatever.

12 While Gallio was proconsul of Achaia (modern Greece), the Jews of Corinth made a united attack on Paul and brought him to be judged. Gallio was a brother to Seneca, who was a tutor of Nero. He was a Roman handled disputes concerning the law, but he was not a religious judge. As a proconsul, he had high connections in Rome. It was right after Gallio's appointment that the Jews brought the case to him. They expected a favorable verdict from Gallio since Judaism was a recognized religion there.

13 "This man," they charged, "is persuading the people to worship God in ways contrary to the law." The Jews in unity accused Paul before Gallio. The illegality of their charge had to do with Jewish, not Roman law. As John MacArthur said, "This was a charge with far-reaching implications. Had Gallio ruled in the Jews' favor, Christianity could have been banned not only in Corinth but also throughout the Empire."[2]

14,15 Just as Paul was about to speak and defend himself, Gallio felt that no defense was necessary. Gallio said to them, "If you Jews were making a complaint about some misdemeanor or serious crime, it would be reasonable for me to listen to you. But since it involves questions about words and names and your own law—settle the matter yourselves. I will not be a judge of such things." Cases of injustice and violence could be handled by Gallio. But Gallio felt that the matter was a Jewish religious dispute which should be settled among themselves.

16 Gallio had made up his mind. He did not want to be involved in the religious matter. He saw this as a distraction from his pressing, more important duties. So he drove off the Jews accusing Paul. Today, we hear a lot about separation of church and state. The church should not meddle in secular things, while the government should not interfere with the religious matters.

17 The Jews accusing Paul had been thrown out of court. Then the crowd there turned on Sosthenes the synagogue leader and beat him up in front of the proconsul. But Gallio showed no concern whatever. Apparently, Sosthenes had replaced Crispus as the ruler of the synagogue. It is not really clear why Sosthenes was beaten. Some suggest that he was the main spokesperson laying the charges against Paul. The Greeks beat him as a way of showing their disapproval of the Jews' action. Apparently, Sosthenes was beaten by his fellow Jews for not representing them well before Gallio.

NOTES

1. John Phillips, *Exploring Acts* (Grand Rapids, MI: Kregel Publications, 1986), p. 355.
2. John MacArthur, *The MacArthur New Testament Commentary: Acts 13-28* (Chicago, IL: Moody Publishers, 1996), p. 152.

CHAPTER 14

PAUL IN TRANSITION

Acts 18:18-28

Paul Returns to Antioch

Verses 18-22: Paul stayed on in Corinth for some time. Then he left the brothers and sisters and sailed for Syria, accompanied by Priscilla and Aquila. Before he sailed, he had his hair cut off at Cenchreae because of a vow he had taken. ¹⁹ They arrived at Ephesus, where Paul left Priscilla and Aquila. He himself went into the synagogue and reasoned with the Jews. ²⁰ When they asked him to spend more time with them, he declined. ²¹ But as he left, he promised, "I will come back if it is God's will." Then he set sail from Ephesus. ²² When he landed at Caesarea, he went up to Jerusalem and greeted the church and then went down to Antioch.

18 Paul stayed on in Corinth for some time. At some point he felt led to return to Syria. Then he left the brothers and sisters and sailed for Syria, accompanied by Priscilla and Aquila. For some unknown reason, Paul had taken a Nazarite vow (Numbers 6:1-21) while in Corinth. This vow involved abstaining from wine, avoiding impurity and immorality, and leaving one's hair uncut. Before he sailed, he had his hair cut off at Cenchreae (the eastern seaport of Corinth) because of a vow he had taken. Cutting off his hair indicated that the Nazarite vow was terminated. It was necessary to complete the vow in Jerusalem. A vow is made only to God and it reveals one's realization of complete dependence on God's will.

19 The three of them arrived at Ephesus, the most important commercial center in Asia Minor. It was also the capital of the Roman province of Asia. The temple of Diana, one of the seven wonders of the ancient world, resided there. The Holy Spirit had earlier forbidden Paul from going to Asia and thus Ephesus (Acts 16:6). Now the timing was right. There Paul left Priscilla and Aquila (note the change in the order of the names). As usual, Paul himself went into the synagogue and reasoned with the Jews about Christ. Aquila and Priscilla were able to follow up and provide a solid base for Paul's future outreach.

20 His visit there was brief. When they asked him to spend more time with them at Ephesus, he declined. Paul refused to extend his stay in the city in spite of the favorable reception. Paul's desire to reach the world with the gospel would not let him stay in one place for too long. He planned to visit Jerusalem to complete his vow and visit Antioch to report to his home church. He left the church at Ephesus in the capable hands of Aquila and Priscilla.

21 Some manuscripts add, "I must by all means be at Jerusalem for the holiday" (TLB). Paul's mind was set on getting to Jerusalem. But as he left, he promised, "I will come back if it is God's will." Though Paul desired to come back, it would only happen if it was God's will. Knowing and doing God's will is important for every believer. Then he set sail from Ephesus.

22 When he landed at Caesarea, a major seaport in Palestine or Canaan and the Roman capital of Judea, he went up to Jerusalem and greeted the church. He possibly told them how he implemented the instructions of the Council of Acts 15. He did not stay long in Jerusalem because his ministry was not there. Then he went down to Antioch and reported all God had used him to accomplish during his second missionary journey. The terms "went up" and "went down" are used to describe the journey to and from Jerusalem and indicate the geographical elevation of the city. Paul had left the brethren about two years ago and they were overjoyed to have him back.

Paul's Third Journey Begins

Verses 23-28: After spending some time in Antioch, Paul set out from there and traveled from place to place throughout the region of Galatia and Phrygia, strengthening all the disciples. [24] *Meanwhile a Jew named Apollos, a native of Alexandria, came to Ephesus. He was a learned man, with a thorough knowledge of the Scriptures.* [25] *He had been instructed in the way of the Lord, and he spoke with great fervor and taught about Jesus accurately, though he knew only the baptism of John.* [26] *He began to speak boldly in the synagogue. When Priscilla and Aquila heard him, they invited him to their home and explained to him the way of God more adequately.* [27] *When Apollos wanted to go to Achaia, the brothers and sisters encouraged him and wrote to the disciples there to welcome him. When he arrived, he was a great help to those who by grace had believed.* [28] *For he vigorously refuted his Jewish opponents in public debate, proving from the Scriptures that Jesus was the Messiah.*

23 After spending some time in Antioch, Paul set out from there and traveled from place to place throughout the region of Galatia and Phrygia, strengthening all the disciples. Galatia was not a city but a region which included such specific cities such as Derbe, Lystra, and Iconium. As a missionary, Paul's heart was always restlessly in the field. His goal was getting to Ephesus. The motivation was to make good on his promise to return there (v. 21). Luke begins the record of Paul's third missionary journey. He interjects with what happened at Ephesus after Paul had left.

24 Meanwhile a Jew named Apollos, a native of Alexandria in Egypt, came to Ephesus. Alexandria was built in 323 B.C. by Alexander the Great, who named the city after himself. The city had a great university and the largest library of its day. "Alexandria, situated on the Nile delta in Egypt, was the second largest city in the Roman Empire… It was at Alexandria that the Hebrew Scriptures were translated into the Greek Septuagint version…. Such was the birthplace of Apollos."[1] Apollos was a learned man, with a thorough knowledge of the Scriptures. He was eloquent and mighty in the Scriptures.

25 He had been instructed in the way of the Lord, and he spoke with great fervor and taught about Jesus accurately, though he knew only the baptism of John. He was already a Christian and a great enthusiast of the faith. Based on his limited knowledge, he was passionate about the way of Christ. Although his teaching was accurate, Apollos' knowledge about Jesus needed to be supplemented. He did not know about the baptism of the Holy Spirit, which occurred on the day of Pentecost.

26 He began to speak boldly in the synagogue. When Priscilla and Aquila heard him, they invited him to their home and explained to him the way of God more adequately. The husband-and-wife team could observe some gaps or deficiencies in Appolos' message, but they did not correct him in public. Priscilla and Aquila invited Apollos to their home and lovingly filled in the gaps related to his knowledge of Christ. Apollos was humble and teachable. The truth always comes to those who are humble enough to be taught.

27 When Apollos wanted to go to Achaia (Corinth), the brothers and sisters encouraged him and wrote to the disciples there to welcome him. (The letter of recommendation is always good for those moving from one place to another.) He was now better equipped for a wider ministry. When he arrived, he was a great help to those who by grace had believed. He helped believers in Corinth develop spiritually through his sound teaching and powerful preaching.

28 Apollos was in Corinth watering what Paul had planted. He vigorously refuted his Jewish opponents in public debate, proving from the OT Scriptures that Jesus was the Messiah. He became so popular that some immature members of the Corinthian church would say, "You may follow Paul, but we follow Apollos" (1 Corinthians 1:12). This attitude created division among the brethren.

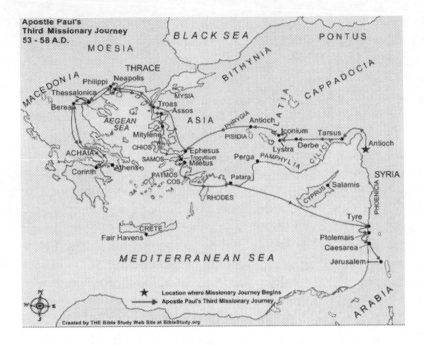

Paul's third missionary journey.

Source: www.biblestudy.org

NOTES

1. John Phillips, *Exploring Acts* (Grand Rapids, MI: Kregel Publications, 1986), p. 374.

CHAPTER 15

PAUL IN EPHESUS

Acts 19:1-22

John's Disciples are Baptized

Verses 1-7: While Apollos was at Corinth, Paul took the road through the interior and arrived at Ephesus. There he found some disciples ² and asked them, "Did you receive the Holy Spirit when you believed?" They answered, "No, we have not even heard that there is a Holy Spirit." ³ So Paul asked, "Then what baptism did you receive?" "John's baptism," they replied. ⁴ Paul said, "John's baptism was a baptism of repentance. He told the people to believe in the one coming after him, that is, in Jesus." ⁵ On hearing this, they were baptized in the name of the Lord Jesus. ⁶ When Paul placed his hands on them, the Holy Spirit came on them, and they spoke in tongues and prophesied. ⁷ There were about twelve men in all.

1 Luke provides the parenthetical account of Apollos. He now continues on his hero's third missionary journey. While Apollos was at Corinth, Paul took the road through the interior and arrived at Ephesus. He was keeping his promise to return to Ephesus (Acts 18:21). There he found some disciples (about twelve, v. 7). These disciples might be disciples of John the Baptist. Their understanding of the Christian faith was similar to that of Apollos before he met Aquila and Priscilla in the previous chapter.

2 Paul asked them, "Did you receive the Holy Spirit when you believed?" Receiving the Holy Spirit is really what makes one a Christian (Romans

8:9). They answered, "No, we have not even heard that there is a Holy Spirit." They were completely ignorant of the existence of the Holy Spirit. They knew nothing about the baptism and indwelling of the Spirit. They did not fully understand what Jesus did.

3 So Paul asked them another basic question: "Then what baptism did you receive?" He asked them the question because a person's baptismal experience indicates his spiritual experience. "John's baptism," they replied. What prompted Paul to ask these questions? Perhaps Paul noticed they were lacking joy or love. There was something that was missing in them.

4 Paul said, "John's baptism was a baptism of repentance. He told the people to believe in the one coming after him, that is, in Jesus." He explained to them that John's baptism looked for the arrival of the Messiah. John himself told the people that they should believe in the One coming after him, Jesus. The twelve men were basically OT saints looking forward to the coming of the Messiah, but the Messiah had come.

5 On hearing this, an adequate explanation was given, and the men were baptized in the name of Jesus Christ Jesus. We are not told that Apollos was baptized again, even though he knew about John's baptism (Acts 18:25). Based on what Paul later wrote, it might be some associate of Paul who did the baptism. This is the only place in the NT where people were rebaptized.

6 When Paul placed his hands on them, the Holy Spirit came on them. As an evidence that the Spirit had come into their lives, they spoke in tongues and prophesied. Speaking in tongues is not the only evidence of a person being filled with the Holy Spirit; it is just one evidence. Other evidences are increased love for Jesus, love for the brethren, zeal for the Lord, and boldness for the Lord.

"This was a mini-Pentecost. We see the Pentecost experience four times in the book of Acts: to *Jewish* believers in Jerusalem, to the *Samaritans* through Philip, to the *Gentiles* by Peter, and here to *dispersed Jews* through Paul"(italic his).[1] Notice that the Holy Spirit comes to every heart at salvation. He makes one a Christian and part of the body of Christ.

7 There were about twelve men in all. This is added as a footnote and the number does not have any symbolic significance. The men praised God and exalted Jesus Christ. They now had what was missing in their lives. "The norm of Christian experience, then, is a cluster of four things: repentance, faith in Jesus, water baptism and the gift of the Spirit."[2] These men would experience a new level of joy, zeal, and love for the Lord and others.

Miracles through Paul

Verses 8-12: Paul entered the synagogue and spoke boldly there for three months, arguing persuasively about the kingdom of God. ⁹ But some of them became obstinate; they refused to believe and publicly maligned the Way. So Paul left them. He took the disciples with him and had discussions daily in the lecture hall of Tyrannus. ¹⁰ This went on for two years, so that all the Jews and Greeks who lived in the province of Asia heard the word of the Lord. ¹¹ God did extraordinary miracles through Paul, ¹² so that even handkerchiefs and aprons that had touched him were taken to the sick, and their illnesses were cured and the evil spirits left them.

8 Paul entered the synagogue and spoke boldly there for the next three months, arguing persuasively about the kingdom of God. He had an open door in the Ephesian synagogue for those three months, which was longer than usual. During that time, he challenged the unbelieving Jews about their religious system. He called them to repentance and to trust in Jesus as their Lord and Messiah. He taught about the kingdom of God, which includes Christ's reign on the earth.

9 Some were persuaded by Paul's preaching. But some of them became obstinate; they refused to believe and publicly maligned the Way. So Paul left the synagogue and moved to a neutral ground. He took the disciples with him and had discussions daily in the lecture hall of Tyrannus. He would work as a tentmaker early in the day and spend the rest of the day teaching the Word of God.

10 This went on for two years, so that all the Jews and Greeks who lived in the province of Asia heard the word of the Lord. While Paul was ministering in Ephesus, the entire province of Asia was evangelized. It was probably during this time that the church at Colossae as well as the churches of Revelation 2-3 was founded. "Two factors made this possible: the witness of the believers as they went from place to place, and the 'special miracles' that God enabled Paul to perform in Ephesus (Acts 19:11)."[3]

11,12 To show that Paul's message was from the Lord, God did extraordinary miracles through Paul. Even handkerchiefs and aprons that had touched him were taken to the sick, and their illnesses were cured and the evil spirits left them. The handkerchief was the cloth Paul used to wipe sweat from his face while working as tentmaker. The aprons were the cloths he put on while working to keep his clothes clean. Paul could not be everywhere, but his handkerchiefs and aprons could go to the places and minister remote healings. The miracles, signs, and wonders were designed to authenticate Paul's ministry.

Some claim that such miraculous healing was only for the apostles. This is nothing but the enemy's lie. God has not changed and Jesus is the same yesterday, today, and forever (Hebrews 13:8). If God needed to authenticate Paul's message, He needs to do the same for our message. I would not be a Christian today if there were no miracles.

Seven Sons of Sceva

Verses 13-16: Some Jews who went around driving out evil spirits tried to invoke the name of the Lord Jesus over those who were demon-possessed. They would say, "In the name of the Jesus whom Paul preaches, I command you to come out." [14] Seven sons of Sceva, a Jewish chief priest, were doing this. [15] One day the evil spirit answered them, "Jesus I know, and Paul I know about, but who are you?" [16] Then the man who had the evil spirit jumped on them and overpowered them all. He gave them such a beating that they ran out of the house naked and bleeding.

13 While the ancient world strongly believed in the existence of demons, many in our modern skeptical age deny it. Some Jews who went around driving out evil spirits tried to invoke the name of the Lord Jesus over those who were demon-possessed. Like Simon of Acts 8, the vagabond Jewish exorcists of Ephesus thought the power of the Spirit could be manipulated somehow. They would say, "In the name of the Jesus whom

Paul preaches, I command you to come out." A secondhand relationship with Jesus is not allowed. God has no grandchildren. We must have a personal relationship with Christ.

14 The seven sons of Sceva, a Jewish chief priest, were trying to do this. Sceva was possibly a member of an aristocratic, priestly family living in Ephesus. They made a living by driving out demons. They must have watched Paul command demons to leave people. They would soon learn that the name of Jesus is no magical charm and that God's authority cannot be evoked by those who do not know Him personally.

15 One day the evil spirit answered them, "Jesus I know, and Paul I know about, but who are you?" They could not fool the evil spirit. The demon knew who Jesus was and trembled at His name. They realized that He is the Holy One of God. They knew Paul too and recognized the authority delegated to him. But the demon challenged the authority of the exorcists over him.

16 Then the man who had the evil spirit jumped on them and overpowered the seven exorcists. He gave them such a beating that they ran out of the house naked and bleeding. They fled for their lives. Their attempt to carelessly meddle in the spiritual realm backfired. In the end, the result was more than what they had hoped for. Their attempt to confront the evil spirits was a complete failure. They were humbled and discredited.

Confession of Sin

*Verses 17-20: When this became known to the Jews and Greeks living in Ephesus, they were all seized with fear, and the name of the Lord Jesus was held in high honor. *[18]* Many of those who believed now came and openly confessed what they had done. *[19]* A number who had practiced sorcery brought their scrolls together and burned them publicly. When they calculated the value of the scrolls, the total came to fifty thousand drachmas. *[20]* In this way the word of the Lord spread widely and grew in power.*

17 When this became known to the Jews and Greeks living in Ephesus, they were all seized with fear, and the name of the Lord Jesus was held in high honor. They recognized that Jesus' name was not be trifled with. On the contrary, Jesus was someone before whom they should bow down in worship. There is power in the glorious name of Jesus.

18 The process of separation from paganism to the Christian experience was helped by what happened. Many of those who believed now came and openly confessed what they had done. Some even divulged their secret occult practices. They came to realize that those practices were useless and sinful. Publicly confessing their sins indicated genuine repentance.

19 A number who had practiced sorcery brought their scrolls together and burned them publicly. When they calculated the value of the scrolls, the total came to fifty thousand drachmas. We don't know how much that is. Someone has estimated it to be over a million dollars in today's currency. Making a break with evil practices was costly. Today there is a renewed interest in spiritism, witchcraft, astrology, and Satanism. But God has forbidden participating in these evil practices (Deuteronomy 18:9-12). He sees them as spiritual adultery.

20 In this way the Word of the Lord spread widely and grew in power. The Word had a wonderful effect on the Ephesians. The Word of God increased among them. It kept growing and gaining strength. The name of the Lord was magnified and His Word spread more rapidly. The public confession led to many conversions.

Paul's Plan

Verses 21,22: After all this had happened, Paul decided to go to Jerusalem, passing through Macedonia and Achaia. "After I have been there," he said, "I must visit Rome also." [22] He sent two of his helpers, Timothy and Erastus, to Macedonia, while he stayed in the province of Asia a little longer.

21 After all this had happened, Paul decided to go to Jerusalem. He made a plan to visit Jerusalem after spending three years in Ephesus. He passed through Macedonia and Achaia, visiting the churches there and collecting offering for the poor believers in Jerusalem. "After I have been there," he said, "I must visit Rome also." Paul's ultimate goal was Rome, not Jerusalem. He must communicate the gospel to those at the center of political power at that time. He was planning to also reach Spain with the gospel of Jesus.

22 He sent two of his helpers, Timothy and Erastus, ahead to Macedonia, while he stayed in the province of Asia a little longer. Paul sent his disciples to Macedonia and Achaia to prepare believers there for his coming. Timothy was Paul's spiritual son and he was with Paul when the churches in Macedonia were established. So they already knew him. Erastus might be the person Paul referred to in Romans 16:23 as the city treasurer.

NOTES

1. R. Kent Hughes, *Acts: The Church Afire* (Wheaton, IL: Crossway, 1996), p. 280.
2. John R. W. Stott, *The Message of Acts* (Downers Grove, IL: IVP Academic, 1990), p. 305.
3. Warren W. Wiersbe, *Be Daring: Acts 13-28* (Colorado Springs, CO: David C. Cook, 1988), p. 87.

CHAPTER 16

RIOT IN EPHESUS

Acts 19:23-41

Opposition by the Silversmiths

Verses 23-27: About that time there arose a great disturbance about the Way. ²⁴ A silversmith named Demetrius, who made silver shrines of Artemis, brought in a lot of business for the craftsmen there. ²⁵ He called them together, along with the workers in related trades, and said: "You know, my friends, that we receive a good income from this business. ²⁶ And you see and hear how this fellow Paul has convinced and led astray large numbers of people here in Ephesus and in practically the whole province of Asia. He says that gods made by human hands are no gods at all. ²⁷ There is danger not only that our trade will lose its good name, but also that the temple of the great goddess Artemis will be discredited; and the goddess herself, who is worshiped throughout the province of Asia and the world, will be robbed of her divine majesty."

23 About that time, just before Paul left Ephesus, there arose a great disturbance about the Way. The early church was identified as the Way. "Christianity is a way of life."[1] Jesus is the way to the Father (John 14:6). After a period of peace and growth, the gospel became offensive to the city's craftsmen. The enemy stirred up human agents and opposed the spread of the gospel.

24 The main person responsible for the disturbance was a silversmith named Demetrius. He was the troublemaking ringleader of the disturbance. He made silver shrines of the goddess Artemis and brought in a lot of business for the craftsmen there. The Artemis (also called Diana) was worshipped throughout the Roman empire as the female goddess of fertility. The impact of the gospel was so strong that sales of idols had fallen drastically in the city of Ephesus. The gospel challenges idolatries of our time: money, sex, power, pleasure, fame, etc. To give your heart to anything other than the true God is idolatry.

25 Realizing the rejection of idol worship by the Christian faith that was spreading rapidly throughout the province, Demetrius decided to act before it was too late. He called his fellow silversmiths together, along with the workers in related trades. He said: "You know, my friends, that we receive a good income from this business." Their main concern was financial; their livelihood was at stake. They were promoting idolatry to make a living.

26 "And you see and hear how this fellow Paul has convinced and led astray large numbers of people here in Ephesus and in practically the whole province of Asia. He says that gods made by human hands are no gods at all." "Nothing will whip up passions more quickly than religion. Just let people get the idea that their religion is threatened, and there is no limit to the lengths they will go."[2]

27 "There is danger not only that our trade will lose its good name, but also that the temple of the great goddess Artemis will be discredited; and the goddess herself, who is worshiped throughout the province of Asia and the world, will be robbed of her divine majesty." Demetrius was concerned about three things. First, their trade would lose its good name. There was the danger of their line of business getting a bad name. Second, the temple of Artemis would be discredited. The temple was one of the seven wonders of the ancient world. It was the glory and pride of the Ephesians. Third, the goddess would be robbed of her majesty. Whatever tarnished the goddess' reputation would lower Ephesus' status. People react when righteousness threatens unrighteousness.

Mob Seizes Paul's Companions

Verses 28-31: When they heard this, they were furious and began shouting: "Great is Artemis of the Ephesians!" [29] Soon the whole city was in an uproar.

The people seized Gaius and Aristarchus, Paul's traveling companions from Macedonia, and all of them rushed into the theater together. ³⁰ Paul wanted to appear before the crowd, but the disciples would not let him. ³¹ Even some of the officials of the province, friends of Paul, sent him a message begging him not to venture into the theater.

28 When they heard Demetrius' powerful speech, they were furious and began shouting: "Great is Artemis of the Ephesians!" Ephesus was in trouble because Artemis (or Diana) had been challenged. Demetrius had succeeded in getting people worried about their pocketbooks and stirring the crowd into a frenzy. The crowd caught fire and their anger knew no bounds. While yelling and screaming, they made their way to the theater.

29 The silversmiths apparently incited people in the streets to riot. Soon the whole city was in an uproar. They could not find Paul; his partners would suffice. The people seized Gaius and Aristarchus (a native of Thessalonica), Paul's traveling companions from Macedonia, and all of them rushed into the theater together. The theater was a regular place for town meetings. It could seat about twenty-five thousand people.

30,31 It was not Paul's style to run away from trouble. He wanted to appear before the crowd and preach to them, but the disciples would not let him. He probably was trying to save his companions from Macedonia. Even some of the officials of the province, friends of Paul, sent him a message begging him not to venture into the theater. Apparently, Paul's message had penetrated into all levels of society, giving him friends in high places.

Paul's disciples and friends urged him not to go to the theater for safety reasons. To show himself to the crowd would definitely mean his death. He might be referring to this riot when he wrote that he fought with beasts at Ephesus (1 Corinthians 15:32).

The Unthinking Mob

Verses 32-34: The assembly was in confusion: Some were shouting one thing, some another. Most of the people did not even know why they were there. ³³ The Jews in the crowd pushed Alexander to the front, and they shouted instructions to him. He motioned for silence in order to make a defense before the people. [34] *But when they realized he was a Jew, they all shouted in unison for about two hours: "Great is Artemis of the Ephesians!"*

32 "The assembly was in confusion: Some were shouting one thing, some another." Most of the people did not even know what was happening or why they were there; they did not understand what the problem was. They were caught up in the excitement of the commotion. Mobs often show the same kind of disorder and confusion. The assembly was somewhat disorganized.

33 The Jews in the crowd pushed a man named Alexander to the front, and they shouted instructions to him. He was put forward as a spokesperson for the Jews. They wanted him to disassociate Paul's message from the Jewish community. It was not the Jews but the Christians who were responsible for the economic problems for the silversmiths. Alexander motioned for silence in order to make a defense before the people.

34 But when they realized he was a Jew, they were not ready to listen to him. Racial prejudice soon entered the picture. To the pagan crowd, there was no difference between Jews and Christians since both rejected idolatry. The crowd shouted in unison for about two hours: "Great is Artemis of the Ephesians!" Their chants were pleas for Artemis to intervene, but she never did. They could shout the slogans as long as they wanted, but the temple of Artemis would come to ruin.

The Clerk Dismisses the Mob

Verses 35-41: The city clerk quieted the crowd and said: "Fellow Ephesians, doesn't all the world know that the city of Ephesus is the guardian of the temple of the great Artemis and of her image, which fell from heaven? [36] *Therefore, since these facts are undeniable, you ought to calm down and not do anything rash.* [37] *You have brought these men here, though they have neither robbed temples nor blasphemed our goddess.* [38] *If, then, Demetrius and his fellow craftsmen have a grievance against anybody, the courts are open and there are proconsuls. They can press charges.* [39] *If there is anything further you want to bring up, it must be settled in a legal assembly.* [40] *As it is, we are in danger of being charged with rioting because of what happened*

*today. In that case we would not be able to account for this commotion, since
there is no reason for it."* [41] *After he had said this, he dismissed the assembly.*

35 The city clerk was an administrative officer (possibly equivalent to our
modern day mayor) who would be held responsible for what happened.
He was able to restore order after two hours of shouting and yelling. He
said to the crowd: "Fellow Ephesians, doesn't all the world know that the
city of Ephesus is the guardian of the temple of the great Artemis and of
her image, which fell from heaven?" He reiterated what everybody already
knew. Everybody knew that Ephesus was the home of Artemis. Everyone
knew that her image came down from heaven. This was probably a stone
that had fallen from the sky. An image might have been carved from a
meteorite and worshiped as divine.

36 "Therefore, since these facts are undeniable, you ought to calm down
and not do anything rash." It was useless and foolish to precipitate a
riot about that from which no harm could come. Therefore, it should
not make any difference what Paul and his companions taught. They
should not fear the intrusion of Christianity. They should let law and
order prevail. Their assembly was unlawful. Rome would not tolerate riots
in the city.

37 "You have brought these men here, though they have neither robbed
temples nor blasphemed our goddess." In spite of Demetrius' claims, the
Christians had done nothing wrong. They were neither temple robbers
nor blasphemers of their goddess. It was Demetrius who had broken the
law by inciting the mob. This meant that the Christians could continue
spreading the gospel unopposed by the authorities.

38 "If, then, Demetrius and his fellow craftsmen have a grievance against
anybody, the courts are open and there are proconsuls. They can press
charges." In other words, rather than inciting a mob, Demetrius should
go through the legal channels and press charges if he had something
against the Christians. Each province had a proconsul or judge who
settled disputes and lawsuits.

39 "If there is anything further you want to bring up, it must be settled
in a legal assembly." If there was anything that could not be settled

in the courts, it should be brought to the legal assembly. If there was something which concerned the whole city, it should be brought to the regular meeting of the assembly. Irrational mob violence should give way to appropriate legal due process in the Roman court system.

40 "As it is, we are in danger of being charged with rioting because of what happened today. In that case we would not be able to account for this commotion, since there is no reason for it." The clerk admitted that there was no reason for the riot. He was apparently a man of great intelligence. He was able to calm the riot and control the crowd.

41 After he had said this, the city clerk dismissed the assembly. Their anger melted away. This was another victory for Paul and his companions. As always, God is in control. The city of Ephesus and the temple are gone, but the gospel and the church of God still remain there. The riot convinced Paul that it was time to leave Ephesus for another place.

NOTES

1. Lloyd J. Ogilvie, *Acts: The Communicator's Commentary* (Waco, TX: Word Books, 1983), p. 284.
2. John Phillips, *Exploring Acts* (Grand Rapids, MI: Kregel Publications, 1986), p. 389.

CHAPTER 17

PAUL'S JOURNEY FROM EPHESUS TO MILETUS

Acts 20:1-16

Paul in Macedonia and Greece

Verses 1-5: When the uproar had ended, Paul sent for the disciples and, after encouraging them, said goodbye and set out for Macedonia. ² He traveled through that area, speaking many words of encouragement to the people, and finally arrived in Greece, ³ where he stayed three months. Because some Jews had plotted against him just as he was about to sail for Syria, he decided to go back through Macedonia. ⁴ He was accompanied by Sopater son of Pyrrhus from Berea, Aristarchus and Secundus from Thessalonica, Gaius from Derbe, Timothy also, and Tychicus and Trophimus from the province of Asia. ⁵ These men went on ahead and waited for us at Troas.

1 When the uproar in Ephesus instigated by Demetrius had ended, Paul sent for the disciples. The disciples were those Paul had had under his discipleship and teaching in Ephesus for two years. After encouraging them, he said goodbye. After leaving Ephesus, Paul crossed the Aegean Sea to reach Macedonia. His plan was to travel from Ephesus to Jerusalem through Macedonia.

2 He traveled through that area, speaking many words of encouragement to the people, and finally arrived in Greece. "Paul had two goals in mind as he visited the various churches. His main purpose was to encourage and strengthen the saints so that they might stand true to the Lord and be effective witnesses. He second purpose was to finish taking up the collection for the needed believers in Jerusalem."[1]

3 He stayed three months in Greece, mostly in Corinth. This was probably during winter months when traveling would be difficult. While at Corinth, Paul wrote his epistle to the Romans. Because some Jews had plotted against him just as he was about to sail for Syria, he decided to go back through Macedonia, visiting the churches there. The Jews wanted to kill Paul because of his successful ministry to the Gentiles. They hated him and his "dangerous" doctrines. Paul was forced to change his plan, but we know that "in all things God works for the good of those who love him" (Romans 8:28).

4 This time, Paul did not travel alone. He was accompanied by Sopater son of Pyrrhus from Berea, Aristarchus and Secundus from Thessalonica, Gaius from Derbe, Timothy, and Tychicus and Trophimus from the province of Asia. These seven men appear only here in Acts except Timothy and Aristarchus. Apart from Timothy, these men were official representatives or delegates of their churches. They had collected offerings for the poor saints in Jerusalem. Having them deliver the contributions gave the contributions a personal touch. It also strengthened the unity between the Jews and Gentiles.

5 These seven men went on ahead and waited for us (the rest of the party) at Troas, where Paul would spend some time and use the opportunity to minister to the believers there again. Luke's use of "us" indicates that he joined Paul at Philippi. Luke had remained in that city when Paul and Silas were forced to leave due to persecution. He made Philippi the center of his work for five or six years.

Paul in Troas

Verses 6-12: But we sailed from Philippi after the Festival of Unleavened Bread, and five days later joined the others at Troas, where we stayed seven days. [7] On the first day of the week we came together to break bread. Paul spoke to the people and, because he intended to leave the next day, kept on talking until midnight. [8] There were many lamps in the upstairs room where we were meeting. [9] Seated in a window was a young man named Eutychus, *who was sinking into a deep sleep as Paul talked on and on. When he was sound asleep, he fell to the ground from the third story and was picked up dead. ¹⁰ Paul went down, threw himself on the young man and put his arms around him. "Don't be alarmed," he said. "He's alive!" ¹¹ Then he went upstairs again and broke bread and ate. After talking until daylight, he left. ¹² The people took the young man home alive and were greatly comforted.*

6 But we (Paul, Luke, and probably Titus) sailed from Philippi after the Festival of Unleavened Bread, and five days later joined the others (the seven church delegates) in Troas, where we stayed seven days. The Jews celebrated the Festival of Unleavened Bread right after the Passover. It is mentioned here simply as a calendar marker.

Luke now joined the group. The last "we" section was Acts 16:10-40. Luke's ministry to Paul helped alleviate the problem associated with his constant traveling.

7 On the first day of the week, we came together to break bread. Notice that this was not the Sabbath (Saturday), but on Sunday. This shows that the early church gathered for worship on Sunday because Jesus rose on Sunday. In this case, they gathered together on Sunday to partake of the Lord's Supper. Paul spoke to the people and, because he intended to leave the next day, kept on talking until midnight. He had so much to say and he simply ignored the clock.

8 There were many lamps in the upstairs room where we were meeting. The place was packed and well lighted with torches and candles. There must have been a lot of smoke in the room due to the lamps and body heat due to the crowd. The room was probably warm which might have made people fall asleep. Also, Paul could prolong his preaching because there was plenty of light from the lamps.

9 Seated in a window was a young man named Eutychus, who was sinking into a deep sleep as Paul talked on and on. Eurychus' spirit was willing but his body was weak. He tried concentrating on Paul's message but he was overcome by drowsiness. When he was sound asleep, he fell to the ground from the third story. He was killed by the fall and was picked up as a corpse. Poor Eutychus!

10 Paul's message was abruptly interrupted. He went down, threw himself on the young man and put his arms around him. This was similar to what Elijah (1 Kings 17:21) and Elisha (2 Kings 4:34) did—they stretched themselves on dead boys and brought them back to life. "Don't be alarmed," Paul said. "He's alive!" A miracle happened. Life returned to the corpse. Eutychus' life was restored. Jesus is still in the business of performing miracles today; all He needs is an instrument to use.

11 Then Paul went upstairs to the third-story room again and broke bread and ate. He was tender and sensitive. He turned their thoughts to a meal. He had a Communion service with them. By sharing a meal and eating together, the church enjoyed fellowship. Paul continued his long sermon, which might seem too long by modern standards. There might be some issues these believers wanted Paul to address. After talking until daylight, he departed.

12 The people took the young man home alive. He was brought to the meeting room in a normal condition. The church was greatly comforted and encouraged. The young man's recovery cheered up everyone. They would remember Paul for good, especially for the amazing miracle. Paul left them as a victor over death.

Paul in Miletus

Verses 13-16: We went on ahead to the ship and sailed for Assos, where we were going to take Paul aboard. He had made this arrangement because he was going there on foot. ^{14} When he met us at Assos, we took him aboard and went on to Mitylene. ^{15} The next day we set sail from there and arrived off Chios. The day after that we crossed over to Samos, and on the following day arrived at Miletus. ^{16} Paul had decided to sail past Ephesus to avoid spending time in the province of Asia, for he was in a hurry to reach Jerusalem, if possible, by the day of Pentecost.

13 We went on ahead to the ship and sailed for Assos, which was about twenty miles south of Troas. There we were going to take Paul aboard. He had made this arrangement because he was going there on foot. In other words, Luke and others went ahead to Assos by ship, while Paul got there by land. We are not told why Paul chose to travel by foot.

14 Paul met the rest of the party at Assos, which was a port on the Asian mainland. His friends took him aboard right away and they went on to Mitylene, which was the leading city of the island of Lesbos and was located on its southeastern coast. Paul did not want to spend too much time in the province of Asia. His mind was set on reaching Jerusalem by the day of Pentecost if possible.

15 The next day we set sail from there and arrived off Chios, which was an island about sixty miles southwest of Mitylene. The day after that we crossed over to Samos, another island about sixty miles southeast of Chios. On the following day, they arrived at Miletus, which was located on the mainland of Asia Minor about thirty miles south of Ephesus. Miletus was a large seaport, where they would probably purchase their provisions for the journey.

16 Paul had decided to sail past Ephesus to avoid spending time in the province of Asia, for he was in a hurry to reach Jerusalem, if possible, by the day of Pentecost, which would be fifty days after the Passover. Why must Paul participate in the Pentecost? Perhaps he would be a Jew to win some Jews to Christ. Or perhaps he wanted to be at Jerusalem to celebrate the birth of the church. Whatever was the reason, being in Jerusalem at Pentecost would allow Paul to meet many unbelievers and reach out to them.

NOTES

1. Warren W. Wiersbe, *Be Daring: Acts 13-28* (Colorado Springs, CO: David C. Cook, 1988), p. 96.

CHAPTER 18

PAUL'S FAREWELL ADDRESS

Acts 20:17-38

Paul's Faithful Service

Verses 17-21: From Miletus, Paul sent to Ephesus for the elders of the church. *[18] When they arrived, he said to them: "You know how I lived the whole time I was with you, from the first day I came into the province of Asia. [19] I served the Lord with great humility and with tears and in the midst of severe testing by the plots of my Jewish opponents. [20] You know that I have not hesitated to preach anything that would be helpful to you but have taught you publicly and from house to house. [21] I have declared to both Jews and Greeks that they must turn to God in repentance and have faith in our Lord Jesus.*

This is the third major speech Paul gave in the Acts. The first speech was addressed to the Jews (Acts 13:16-41), the second one to the Gentiles (Acts 17:22-31), and this one to Christians. Paul's message to the elders can be divided into three parts: relating to the past (vs. 18-11), his future ministry (vs. 22-27), and his present (vs. 28-35).

17 From Miletus, Paul sent to Ephesus for the elders of the church. Since Ephesus was only about thirty miles away from Miletus, the elders could easily come down and meet Paul at Miletus to economize on time. The ship Paul was sailing in remained at Miletus for some days. Paul used that time to address the leaders of the church at Ephesus. These were individuals who were spiritually mature enough to rule the church. Their duties included taking care of the affairs of the church, reaching out to outsiders, and edifying the members.

18 When they arrived, he said to them: "You know how I lived the whole time I was with you, from the first day I came into the province of Asia." The elders had closely observed Paul during his three-year stay with them. They knew about his manner of life. His life and ministry had been an open book. He never lorded it over them or coveted their resources. He was not interested in making money from the ministry. His motive for ministry was spiritual, not selfish. He was selflessly dedicated to serving the needs of others. He did his best to live an exemplary life before the Ephesians.

19 "I served the Lord with great humility and with tears and in the midst of severe testing by the plots of my Jewish opponents." Paul considered his ministry as serving the Lord and himself as a bond-servant of Christ (Romans 1:1, NASB). He served the Lord with great humility. Humility is not thinking of ourselves. "Augustine said to follow Christ's way, the first most important thing was humility, the second most important thing was humility and the third most important thing was humility."[1]

Paul also served with tears, grieving over the lost and sinning believers, and enduring threats posed by false teachers. His ministry was marked by self-sacrifice and faithfulness.

20 "You know that I have not hesitated to preach anything that would be helpful to you but have taught you publicly and from house to house." Paul kept back nothing that would help the Ephesians grow in the Lord. He withheld no teaching that was helpful. He visited people where they were, traveling from house to house. It really did not matter to Paul whether it was a Jewish home or Gentile home.

21 "I have declared to both Jews and Greeks that they must turn to God in repentance and have faith in our Lord Jesus." Paul regarded himself as a herald, proclaiming the Good News to sinners. According to Paul, a gospel message must have two elements. First, it must address repentance to God. Repentance is a change of mind that results in a corresponding change in behavior. Second, a gospel message should include faith in the Lord Jesus Christ. Saving faith involves trusting Christ for salvation. Paul preached the same message for both Jews and Gentiles since everyone is a sinner and has come short the glory of God.

Paul's Willingness to Die

Verses 22-24: "And now, compelled by the Spirit, I am going to Jerusalem, not knowing what will happen to me there. ²³ I only know that in every city the Holy Spirit warns me that prison and hardships are facing me. ²⁴ However, I consider my life worth nothing to me; my only aim is to finish the race and complete the task the Lord Jesus has given me—the task of testifying to the good news of God's grace.

22 "And now, compelled by the Spirit, I am going to Jerusalem, not knowing what will happen to me there." The Lord had told Paul that his testimony would not be well received in Jerusalem. He would be persecuted and arrested. He was going there now, not knowing what would happen to him. Because he stubbornly went to Jerusalem, he spent much of his remaining time in prison. He wrote some epistles while in prison

23 Paul mentioned what he did not know in the previous verse. In this verse, he mentioned what he did know. "I only know that in every city the Holy Spirit warns me that prison and hardships are facing me." It was revealed to Paul that he would face persecution in almost every city. He would endure hardship and suffering for the sake of the gospel (2 Corinthians 11:23-28).

24 "However, I consider my life worth nothing to me; my only aim is to finish the race and complete the task the Lord Jesus has given me—the task of testifying to the good news of God's grace." Paul had a sound attitude. Nothing will stop him from achieving his goal. To Paul what mattered was finishing the work assigned to him by the Lord. He mattered little to him if tribulation awaited him. He would later write Timothy, "I have fought the good fight, I have finished the race, I have kept the faith" (2 Timothy 4:7).

Challenging by Example

Verses 25-35: "Now I know that none of you among whom I have gone about preaching the kingdom will ever see me again. ²⁶ Therefore, I declare to you today that I am innocent of the blood of any of you. ²⁷ For I have not hesitated to proclaim to you the whole will of God. ²⁸ Keep watch over yourselves and all the flock of which the Holy Spirit has made you overseers. Be shepherds of the church of God, which he bought with his own blood. ²⁹ I know that after I leave, savage wolves will come in among you and will not spare the flock. ³⁰ Even from your own number men will arise and distort the truth in order to draw away disciples after them. ³¹ So be on your guard! Remember that for three years I never stopped warning each of you night and day with tears. ³² "Now I commit you to God and to the word of his grace, which can build you up and give you an inheritance among all those who are sanctified. ³³ I have not coveted anyone's silver or gold or clothing. ³⁴ You yourselves know that these hands of mine have supplied my own needs and the needs of my companions. ³⁵ In everything I did, I showed you that by this kind of hard work we must help the weak, remembering the words the Lord Jesus himself said: 'It is more blessed to give than to receive.'"

25 "Now I know that none of you among whom I have gone about preaching the kingdom will ever see me again." Paul was not expecting to be back in Asia Minor, especially Ephesus. He believed he had completed his work there and that they would not meet again. There were millions of people who were yet to hear the gospel. Paul's plan was to reach Rome and the regions beyond.

26 "Therefore, I declare to you today that I am innocent of the blood of any of you." Paul had faithfully declared to them the whole counsel of God. By echoing the prophet Ezekiel's concept of the watchmen, he declared that he was innocent of their blood (Ezekiel 33:7-9) and his conscience was clear. Just as the watchman on the walls in the OT needed to be faithful and sound the alarm if he saw danger approaching, the shepherd must warn sinners and be responsible for edifying the saints.

27 "For I have not hesitated to proclaim to you the whole will of God." Church leaders, elders and pastors, must maintain that same commitment. Proclaiming the whole will of God may mean going through God's Word verse-by-verse. Leaders who fail to present the whole truth would have the people's blood upon their heads. We are to pray for our spiritual leaders since they are accountable to the Lord.

28 "Keep watch over yourselves and all the flock of which the Holy Spirit has made you overseers. Be shepherds of the church of God, which he bought with his own blood." Timothy was asked to pay close attention to himself and his teaching (1 Timothy 4:16). In the same way, church leaders must constantly perform self-examination. They must be good shepherds of the flock of God under their care. They must feed the sheep, care for them, lead them, and protect them.

29 "I know that after I leave, savage wolves will come in among you and will not spare the flock." Paul was sure that after his departure, wolves or false teachers would attack the flock. The coming attack was inevitable. They would distort God's Word for their self-serving ends. Wherever God's work is performed, Satan can be expected to oppose and counter with lies. Church leaders must be equipped to detect and defeat these enemies.

30 "Even from your own number men will arise and distort the truth in order to draw away disciples after them." They should expect attacks from both outside and inside of their local church. Paul had been diligently exposing errors and upholding the truth. The elders were now responsible for doing that. Being an elder in the church of God should not be taken lightly.

31 "So be on your guard! Remember that for three years I never stopped warning each of you night and day with tears." A shepherd must be alert to what is happening around. For the entire three years Paul spent with them, he never ceased warning them about false teachers. He was concerned (to the point of shedding tears) that his people could be deceived by false prophets. The order of the words "night and day" is intended to be hyperbolical (see 1 Thessalonians 2:9).

32 "Now I commit you to God and to the word of his grace, which can build you up and give you an inheritance among all those who are sanctified." As Paul was about to leave, he could do no better than to commend the elders to God, who would not change and who could keep them.

An undershepherd must be committed to studying the Word of God. The Word is able to build up the saints and provide them an inheritance. It is the source of their spiritual growth. God's people today should be guided by the word of His grace.

33 "I have not coveted anyone's silver or gold or clothing." The apostle Paul was a man of integrity like Samuel (1 Samuel 12:3, 4). Paul's ministry was not marked by getting things from others but by sacrificially giving to the needs of others. He had worked among wealthy people, but never coveted their riches. As leaders, we are to let our character be free from the love of money (Hebrews 13:5). We must never covet but trust God who has promised to supply all our needs according to His riches in glory (Philippians 4:19).

34 "You yourselves know that these hands of mine have supplied my own needs and the needs of my companions." Although Paul had a legitimate right to be supported by those who benefited from his ministry, he chose to support himself and his companions through tent making. He wanted to be free from being dependent on people. He made an exception to the biblical principle that those who labor in teaching the Word ought to be supported by the Word (1 Corinthians 9:14).

35 "In everything I did, I showed you that by this kind of hard work we must help the weak, remembering the words the Lord Jesus himself said: 'It is more blessed to give than to receive.'" Paul's life had been exemplary; he set a pace for others to follow. He not only worked to support himself but to help those who were in need or support those who were weak spiritually.

Paul believed what Jesus said (but was not recorded in the gospels) that it is more blessed to give than to receive. Blessing comes from sharing what we have. As James said, "Faith without deeds is dead" (James 2:26). And as Lloyd Ogilvie said, "The more we receive of Him, the more we have to give of what people really need—love, forgiveness, and lasting care."[2]

A Sad Farewell

Verses 36-38: When Paul had finished speaking, he knelt down with all of them and prayed ³⁷ *They all wept as they embraced him and kissed him.* ³⁸ *What grieved them most was his statement that they would never see his face again. Then they accompanied him to the ship.*

36 The saying of Jesus closes Paul's farewell address. When Paul had finished speaking, he knelt down with all of them and prayed. Jesus too knelt down and prayed after His farewell speech (Luke 22:41). Paul prayed with the Ephesian elders because he realized that his farewell address needed to be undergirded by prayer if it was to bear fruit. His prayer is not recorded by Luke. The outward position one assumes while praying is irrelevant. What matters is being humble and dependent on the Lord.

37 When the prayer was over, they all wept as they embraced him and kissed him. The parting was apparently emotional. The display of emotion with tears and kisses (probably on the cheeks) was natural. Those who care and minister to our needs always have a special place in our hearts. We love and appreciate them in return. Nothing creates a closer bond than laboring together in the Lord's vineyard. "Like Paul, all believers can build a strong relationships with other believers, caring, sorrowing, rejoicing, and praying with them."[3]

38 What grieved them most was his statement that they would never see his face again in this life. They felt real pain over the fact that they would never see him again. Their grief expressed their great affection for him. Having said their final good byes, they accompanied him to the ship. With much sadness and determination to be good shepherds as Paul urged them to, they returned home.

NOTES

1. Derek Carlsen, *Faith & Courage: Commentary on Acts* (Arlington Heights, IL: Christian Liberty Press, 2000), p. 449.

2. Lloyd J. Ogilvie, *Acts: The Communicator's Commentary* (Waco, TX: Word Books, 1983), p. 292.
3. Bruce B. Barton et al., *Life Application Bible Commentary: Acts* (Carol Stream, IL: Tyndale House Publishers, 1999), p. 353.

CHAPTER 19

RETURN TO JERUSALEM

Acts 21:1-16

Prophecy at Tyre

Verses 1-6: After we had torn ourselves away from them, we put out to sea and sailed straight to Kos. The next day we went to Rhodes and from there to Patara. ² We found a ship crossing over to Phoenicia, went on board and set sail. ³ After sighting Cyprus and passing to the south of it, we sailed on to Syria. We landed at Tyre, where our ship was to unload its cargo. ⁴ We sought out the disciples there and stayed with them seven days. Through the Spirit they urged Paul not to go on to Jerusalem. ⁵ When it was time to leave, we left and continued on our way. All of them, including wives and children, accompanied us out of the city, and there on the beach we knelt to pray. ⁶ After saying goodbye to each other, we went aboard the ship, and they returned home.

1 After parting with the Ephesian elders, Paul and his companions put out to sea and sailed straight to Kos, which was the capital of the island Kos. The Greek term *apospao* literally means "to tear away," but it is translated as "parted" in RSV and TLB. The next day they went to Rhodes, which was noted for its lighthouse—one of the seven wonders of the ancient world. From there they got to Patara, a busy seaport located on Asia Minor.

2 Paul and his companions were probably not comfortable with a ship that moved slowly and stopped at every port. They found another ship crossing over to Phoenicia, went on board and set sail. It seems that Paul and his party took a larger ship here, one that sails across the sea. Such a ship would accommodate their schedule and speed them on their way to Jerusalem. The journey would take about four hundred miles.

3 After sighting Cyprus and passing to the south of it, we sailed on to Syria. The ship did not stop at Cyprus. We landed at Tyre in Syria. There at the chief city of Phoenicia, their ship was to unload its cargo. (Jesus visited Tyre during his ministry on earth.) This apparent delay did not prevent Paul from being in Jerusalem for the Pentecost (Acts 20:16).

4 The missionaries knew about the church at Tyre. They sought out the disciples there and stayed with them seven days. Through the Spirit they urged Paul not to go on to Jerusalem, but Paul ignored the warning. The warning might have come in form of prophecy. Paul might have been warned of the persecution he would encounter in Jerusalem. In spite of the repeated warnings, Paul's desire to be in Jerusalem could not be deterred. He probably hoped that God would overrule all things no matter what happened at Jerusalem.

5 When it was time to leave, the missionary team left and continued on their way. It was possibly the same ship they had been on before. All of them, including wives and children, accompanied us out of the city, and there on the beach we knelt to pray. It was a moment of fellowship and mutual encouragement. Once at Miletus and now at Tyre, Paul got on his knees to pray corporately with other Christians.

6 The church at Tyre does not seem to be large—they all came to the beach with their wives and children. Like believers in Miletus, the Tyrean Christians were reluctant to bid goodbye. After saying goodbye to each other, Paul and his party went aboard the ship, and the believers from Tyre returned home. This was another separation of disciples who loved each other.

Prophecy at Caesarea

Verses 7-14: We continued our voyage from Tyre and landed at Ptolemais, where we greeted the brothers and sisters and stayed with them for a day.

⁸ Leaving the next day, we reached Caesarea and stayed at the house of Philip the evangelist, one of the Seven. ⁹ He had four unmarried daughters who prophesied. ¹⁰ After we had been there a number of days, a prophet named Agabus came down from Judea. ¹¹ Coming over to us, he took Paul's belt, tied his own hands and feet with it and said, "The Holy Spirit says, 'In this way the Jewish leaders in Jerusalem will bind the owner of this belt and will hand him over to the Gentiles.'" ¹² When we heard this, we and the people there pleaded with Paul not to go up to Jerusalem. ¹³ Then Paul answered, "Why are you weeping and breaking my heart? I am ready not only to be bound, but also to die in Jerusalem for the name of the Lord Jesus." ¹⁴ When he would not be dissuaded, we gave up and said, "The Lord's will be done."

7 Paul and his company continued their voyage from Tyre and landed at Ptolemais, which was about thirty miles from Tyre. They sought for the brothers and sisters in that city and stayed with them for a day. Paul always sought opportunities to meet God's people and share the love of Christ with them. It shows that the church of Christ is one body regardless of location.

8 Leaving the next day, they reached Caesarea after a journey of forty miles. Caesarea was the Roman capital of Palestine or Judea. They stayed at the house of Philip the evangelist, one of the Seven. Philip was one of the seven men (or deacons) who had been selected to distribute food to widows (Acts 6:5, 6). He was the only one called evangelist in Acts. He was the one who first preached the gospel to the Samaritans and later to the Ethiopian eunuch.

9 Philip was blessed with four unmarried daughters who prophesied. They were virgins and prophetesses. Prophets along with apostles, evangelists, teachers, and pastors were (and still are) God's gifts to the church (Ephesians 4:11). These ladies were free to use their gifts within the church. Besides these four prophetesses, prophets like Agabus (Acts 11:28), Judas and Silas (Acts 15:32) were also mentioned in Acts.

10 After we had been there a number of days, a prophet named Agabus came down from Jerusalem in Judea. While staying briefly in Caesarea, Paul met the prophet Agabus. We have met the prophet Agabus before.

At Antioch, he prophesied about an impending worldwide famine (Acts 11:27, 28). Here he was about to foretell a future event as prophets do.

11 Coming over to the apostolic team, he took Paul's belt, and tied his own hands and feet with it. Agabus prophesied, "The Holy Spirit says, 'In this way the Jewish leaders in Jerusalem will bind the owner of this belt and will hand him over to the Gentiles.'" The prophecy coupled with the dramatic action was essentially on Paul's arrest in Jerusalem. Most prophesies begin with "Thus says the Lord," but this one begins with "Thus says the Holy Spirit." The Spirit and the Lord are one. Agabus could only share the prophecy he got from the Lord; he could not make Paul react in a particular way.

12 When the missionaries and other people who were there heard Abagus' prophecy, they pleaded with Paul not to go up to Jerusalem. (Jerusalem had the reputation for killing the prophets sent to her.) Their deep love for the apostle compelled them to beg him not to risk his life. They believed that Paul would face danger in Jerusalem and wanted to preserve him and his vital ministry. We have seen how difficult any guidance through prophecy could be.

13 Then Paul answered, "Why are you weeping and breaking my heart? I am ready not only to be bound, but also to die in Jerusalem for the name of the Lord Jesus." Paul would not be deterred from achieving his goal. He had his reasons for visiting Jerusalem. He was determined to personally deliver the gifts to the Jerusalem church. He was ready for imprisonment or even death.

14 When the brethren realized that Paul had made up his mind, they stopped opposing him. When he would not be dissuaded, they gave up. They handed the matter over to the Lord and said, "The Lord's will be done." Both Paul and his friends must abide in the will of God. That is the ultimate issue. When faced with a situation we cannot change, our best option is to commit it to God's hand.

Arrival at Jerusalem

Verses 15,16: After this, we started on our way up to Jerusalem. ¹⁶ Some of the disciples from Caesarea accompanied us and brought us to the home of Mnason, where we were to stay. He was a man from Cyprus and one of the early disciples.

15 After this, they started the last leg or stage of their journey to Jerusalem. Not able to persuade Paul from changing his mind, the missionaries headed up for Jerusalem. The distance from Caesarea to Jerusalem was about sixty-five miles. Since Caesarea was on a lower elevation than Jerusalem, the people apparently must go up to Jerusalem. They possibly arrived by foot two days before Pentecost.

16 Some of the disciples from Caesarea accompanied the missionaries, possibly to celebrate the feast and protect Paul. They brought them to the home of Mnason, where they were to stay. He was a man from Cyprus and one of the early disciples. He had a house in Jerusalem which was spacious enough to accommodate Paul and the other believers traveling with him.

CHAPTER 20

PAUL IN JERUSALEM

Acts 21:17-40

Paul Reports in Jerusalem

Verses 17-19: When we arrived at Jerusalem, the brothers and sisters received us warmly. [18] *The next day Paul and the rest of us went to see James, and all the elders were present.* [19] *Paul greeted them and reported in detail what God had done among the Gentiles through his ministry.*

17 At last, Paul and his company arrived at Jerusalem, their destination. "Paul's arrival in Jerusalem marked the end of his missionary journeys. He would soon be arrested and remain an 'ambassador in chains' (Eph. 6:20) for the remainder of the period covered by Acts."[1] When the missionaries arrived at Jerusalem, the brothers and sisters (including Mnason) received them warmly. They were apparently pleased with the generous gifts from the Gentile churches.

18 The next day Paul and the rest of the missionaries went to see James, and all the elders were present. This official reception was attended by James, the half-brother of our Lord (Mark 6:3), and other leaders of the Jerusalem church. James was regarded as one of the pillars of the church in Jerusalem. The apostles were not mentioned. It is possible they were out spreading the gospel. This verse marks the last time Luke will use "we" or "us" until Acts 27:1 when he will include himself again.

19 Paul greeted them and reported in detail what God had done among the Gentiles through his ministry. He humbly gave the credit to God. He mentioned one by one what God did through him during his missionary journeys since the Jerusalem Council of Acts 15. This would include the miraculous things God did among the Gentiles, the growth of the churches in Asia, Macedonia, and Achaia, and the increase in the number of Gentile believers.

Encouraging Believers

Verses 20-26: When they heard this, they praised God. Then they said to Paul: "You see, brother, how many thousands of Jews have believed, and all of them are zealous for the law. ²¹ They have been informed that you teach all the Jews who live among the Gentiles to turn away from Moses, telling them not to circumcise their children or live according to our customs. ²² What shall we do? They will certainly hear that you have come, ²³ so do what we tell you. There are four men with us who have made a vow. ²⁴ Take these men, join in their purification rites and pay their expenses, so that they can have their heads shaved. Then everyone will know there is no truth in these reports about you, but that you yourself are living in obedience to the law. ²⁵ As for the Gentile believers, we have written to them our decision that they should abstain from food sacrificed to idols, from blood, from the meat of strangled animals and from sexual immorality."²⁶ The next day Paul took the men and purified himself along with them. Then he went to the temple to give notice of the date when the days of purification would end and the offering would be made for each of them.

20 When the brethren in Jerusalem heard this, they praised and glorified God. They were not jealous but rejoiced in what the Lord was doing through Paul. Then they said to Paul: "You see, brother, how many thousands of Jews have believed, and all of them are zealous for the law." Although a lot of Jews had been converted, most of them still insistently followed the Jewish traditions and customs. Knowing how difficult it was for them to break away from their past, God Himself was tolerant with them during this period of transition.

21 "They have been informed that you teach all the Jews who live among the Gentiles to turn away from Moses, telling them not to circumcise their children or live according to our customs." The Judaizers were Paul's bitter enemies, who followed him wherever he went throughout his missionary journeys. Their accusations of him were false. He nowhere taught that Jewish believers should abandon Mosaic law. These lies had been propagated by the Judaizers and had reached the Jerusalem Jews.

Paul had always endeavored to mend the division between the Jews and the Gentiles. He believed that they belonged to the same body of Christ (Colossians 3:11). Although Paul taught the Gentiles not to be circumcised (1 Corinthians 7:18, 19), he never instructed the Jews to abandon circumcision.

22 "What shall we do? They will certainly hear that you have come." Whether false or not, the accusations were serious and something should be done. The accusers would surely know that Paul was in town. During his long absence from Jerusalem, Paul had interacted with the Gentiles and because of this, the Jews regarded him as ceremoniously unclean. The elders would not like to have a confrontation between Paul and the Jewish zealots. So they devised a plan.

23,24 They now proposed what Paul should do. "There are four men with us who have made a vow. Take these men, join in their purification rites and pay their expenses, so that they can have their heads shaved. Then everyone will know there is no truth in these reports about you, but that you yourself are living in obedience to the law." In addition to paying for the expenses of the four Nazirites, they urged Paul to participate in the purification rites. They hoped that Paul's participation in the Jewish ritual would offset the rumors against him.

The Nazirite vow was a vow of consecration and an institution prescribed in Moses' law (Numbers 6). For a period of time, they would have no wine, no shaving, or no touching of a dead body. At the end of the vow, they would bring some offerings to the temple. Paul was advised to pay the expenses of the offerings for the four men, which was substantial.

25 "As for the Gentile believers, we have written to them our decision that they should abstain from food sacrificed to idols, from blood, from the meat of strangled animals and from sexual immorality." This is a summary of the Jerusalem Council's decision. They were not adding or changing anything in that decision. Nothing in the decision required that the Gentiles should be circumcised. The liberty of the Gentile believers was not touched by the law of Moses.

26 The next day Paul took the men and purified himself along with them. Then he went to the temple to give notice of the date when the days of purification would end and the offering would be made for each of them. The priests at the temple needed advance notice so that adequate preparation could be made. Paul along with the four men had to wait for seven days (v. 27) before offering the prescribed sacrifices.

This should not be regarded as a compromise on the part of Paul. He was humble to take their suggestion and participate in the purification rites. He had taken a Nazirite vow before (Acts 18:18). Participating in it again would not compromise any biblical truth. To the Jews, Paul became a Jew to win some (1 Corinthians 9:20).

Asian Jews Cause a Riot

Verses 27-30: When the seven days were nearly over, some Jews from the province of Asia saw Paul at the temple. They stirred up the whole crowd and seized him, ²⁸ shouting, "Fellow Israelites, help us! This is the man who teaches everyone everywhere against our people and our law and this place. And besides, he has brought Greeks into the temple and defiled this holy place." ²⁹ (They had previously seen Trophimus the Ephesian in the city with Paul and assumed that Paul had brought him into the temple.) ³⁰ The whole city was aroused, and the people came running from all directions. Seizing Paul, they dragged him from the temple, and immediately the gates were shut.

27 When the seven days were nearly over, Paul encountered some opposition from his old fiercest enemies. Some Jews from the province of Asia (possibly Ephesus) saw Paul at the temple. Jews from all over the world would come to Jerusalem for the feasts. The Asian Jews were quite familiar with Paul. His gracious action did not appease them. It provoked the very situation he was trying to avoid. They stirred up the whole crowd and seized him like a criminal.

28 They shouted, "Fellow Israelites, help us! This is the man who teaches everyone everywhere against our people and our law and this place. And besides, he has brought Greeks into the temple and defiled this holy place." The accusation had two components. First, they were saying that Paul was teaching against the Jews, their law, and Jerusalem. They saw Paul as a disloyal, apostate Jew. This was not true, as Paul was showing respect to the Jewish customs. Second, they asserted that Paul had brought Gentiles to defile the temple. He knew the requirement that Gentiles were not allowed to pass the court of the Gentiles. This accusation was not enough to bring people running from all directions (v. 30). False accusation is often easy to make but hard to undo.

29 The basis of their charge was weak. They had previously seen Trophimus the Ephesian (a Gentile) in the city with Paul and assumed that Paul had brought him into the temple. They accused Paul of bringing Gentiles into the proscribed section of the temple that was designated just for the Jews. Paul could not have done this because he knew better. Paul's enemies made an assumption but failed to check the facts.

30 The commotion soon attracted the attention of many others in the city. Most of the residents were in the temple at this time. All the pent-up anger of the pilgrims was turned on Paul. The whole city was aroused, and the people came running from all directions. Seizing Paul, they dragged him from the temple, and immediately the gates were shut. The temple police closed the gates to avoid defilement by the unruly mob. The false accusations of the Asian Jews spread like wildfire. They had achieved their goal.

Paul Rescued by the Romans

Verses 31-40: While they were trying to kill him, news reached the commander of the Roman troops that the whole city of Jerusalem was in an uproar. ³² He at once took some officers and soldiers and ran down to the crowd. When the rioters saw the commander and his soldiers, they stopped beating Paul. ³³ The commander came up and arrested him and ordered him to be bound with two chains. Then he asked who he was and what he had done. ³⁴ Some in the crowd shouted one thing and some another, and since the commander could not get at the truth because of the uproar, he ordered that

Paul be taken into the barracks. ³⁵ When Paul reached the steps, the violence of the mob was so great he had to be carried by the soldiers. ³⁶ The crowd that followed kept shouting, "Get rid of him!"

31 While they were trying to kill him, news reached the commander of the Roman troops that the whole city of Jerusalem was in an uproar. The name of the commander was Claudius Lysias (Acts 23:26). He was responsible for maintaining order in the city. During a feast like this, extra troops were often stationed at the Fortress of Antonia, which was located at the northwest corner of the temple area. The troops were ready for any emergence on a moment's notice.

32 Without wasting time, the commander acted decisively. He at once took some officers and soldiers and ran down to the crowd. When the rioters saw the commander and his soldiers approaching the scene, they stopped beating Paul. The soldiers were armed, while the attackers were not. The massive show of military force quelled the riot and saved Paul's life. Thus, the Roman military brought order to the city.

33 The commander came up and arrested Paul and ordered him to be bound with two chains, confirming Agabus' earlier prophecy. It was obvious to the commander that Paul was the cause of the riot. He assumed Paul was a violent criminal. He arrested him, not his attackers. Then he asked who he was and what he had done. Lysias wanted to know what was the cause of the riot and how Paul was involved or what he did to incite the riot.

34 It was difficult to get any useful information from the crowd. Nobody could reason with the crowd. Some in the crowd shouted one thing and some another. The people gave conflicting answers and could not agree on what the issues were. Since the commander could not get at the truth because of the uproar, he ordered that Paul be taken into the barracks. He intended to interrogate him in private.

35 When Paul reached the stairs, the violence of the mob was so great he had to be carried by the soldiers to protect him. He was fortunate to be protected by the soldiers. The soldiers had to carry Paul from the temple area to the Fortress of Antonia (into the barracks) because of the pressure of the mob. "Paul was now handcuffed to two soldiers. His career as a prisoner had begun. Little did he know that it was to last for years and it would fulfill his fondest dream—to see Rome."[2]

36 The rioters, seeing their prey escaping their grasp, followed the soldiers and tried to get close enough. They kept shouting, "Get rid of him!" Not far from the same location, another angry mob had said the same thing to Pilate regarding Jesus twenty-seven years before (Luke 23:18). There was no question about the motive of the blood-thirsty mob. They wanted Paul dead. They were bent on lynching him.

Paul Wants to Address the Crowd

Verses 37-40: As the soldiers were about to take Paul into the barracks, he asked the commander, "May I say something to you?" "Do you speak Greek?" he replied. [38] "Aren't you the Egyptian who started a revolt and led four thousand terrorists out into the wilderness some time ago?" [39] Paul answered, "I am a Jew, from Tarsus in Cilicia, a citizen of no ordinary city. Please let me speak to the people." [40] After receiving the commander's permission, Paul stood on the steps and motioned to the crowd. When they were all silent, he said to them in Aramaic.

37 As the soldiers were about to take Paul into the barracks, he asked the commander, "May I say something to you?" In reply, the commander asked, "Do you speak Greek?" Greek was the language of the cultured, educated people. It was the lingua franca of the ancient world. Most Palestinians spoke Aramaic (a Hebrew dialect), the language the Jews brought back from Babylonian captivity. Being able to speak Greek gave Paul favor before Lysias and the opportunity to defend himself.

38 Lysias asked Paul, "Aren't you the Egyptian who started a revolt and led four thousand terrorists out into the wilderness some time ago?" His question assumed a positive answer from Paul. "The Egyptian to whom the tribune referred was a false prophet who had led a number of the Sicarii to the Mount of Olives, assuring them that the walls of Jerusalem would fall down before them at his word of command; then they would overpower the Roman garrison and capture Jerusalem."[3] This is not in the Bible, but taken from the record of Josephus, the Jewish historian.

39 Paul answered, "I am a Jew, from Tarsus in Cilicia, a citizen of no ordinary city. Please let me speak to the people." Paul was not an Egyptian as Lysias assumed. As a Jew, he could worship in the temple. He was proud of being a citizen of the great metropolis of Tarsus. It was a famous and prestigious city, which was responsible for Paul's good education and his knowledge of Greek.

40 The commander's plan to interrogate Paul was interrupted by Paul's bold request to address the people. After receiving the commander's permission, Paul stood on the steps and motioned to the crowd. He saw this as an opportunity to speak to the people he loved so much (Romans 9:1-4). In spite of their hatred and rejection, his burning desire was that they might accept Christ as their Lord and Savior. When they were all silent, he spoke to the crowd in Aramaic.

NOTES

1. John MacArthur, *The MacArthur New Testament Commentary: Acts 13-28* (Chicago, IL: Moody Publishers, 1996), p. 247.
2. John Phillips, *Exploring Acts* (Grand Rapids, MI: Kregel Publications, 1986), p. 429.
3. Ibid., p.431.

CHAPTER 21

PAUL'S DEFENSE

Acts 22:1-21

Paul's Background

Verses 1-5: "Brothers and fathers, listen now to my defense." ² When they heard him speak to them in Aramaic, they became very quiet. Then Paul said: ³ "I am a Jew, born in Tarsus of Cilicia, but brought up in this city. I studied under Gamaliel and was thoroughly trained in the law of our ancestors. I was just as zealous for God as any of you are today. ⁴ I persecuted the followers of this Way to their death, arresting both men and women and throwing them into prison, ⁵ as the high priest and all the Council can themselves testify. I even obtained letters from them to their associates in Damascus, and went there to bring these people as prisoners to Jerusalem to be punished.

1 "Brothers and fathers, listen now to my defense." Paul addressed them as "brothers and fathers." Presumably, there were no women and children there. He spoke to them with respect and identified with them. He spoke to them calmly, applying Solomon's words: "A gentle answer turns away wrath" (Proverbs 15:1). His burning desire was to share the gospel with the Jews in Jerusalem. Now he had that opportunity. This was the first of the five defenses or "apologies" the Romans would allow Paul to make.

2 When they heard him speak to them in Aramaic, they became very quiet. Paul was multi-lingual. He talked to the commander in Greek a while ago, but now he was speaking to the crowd in Aramaic, the vernacular of the Middle East. To have someone address us in our mother tongue touches our heart. Speaking in Aramaic helped win him a listening audience.

3 "I am a Jew, born in Tarsus of Cilicia, but brought up in this city. I studied under Gamaliel and was thoroughly trained in the law of our ancestors. I was just as zealous for God as any of you are today." He started with his biographical information. He identified himself as a Jew, declaring his brotherhood with the crowd. Though he was born in Tarsus, he was brought up right there, in Jerusalem. Having been a student of the famous Gamaliel (Acts 5:34), he was thoroughly trained in the Jewish laws and customs. He was zealous for God just as they were today. How could they not listen to a man with that credential?

4 In his great zeal for God, Paul persecuted the followers of this Way to their death, arresting both men and women and throwing them into prison. His persecution of Christians showed the zeal that characterized his life at that time. His goal back then was to stamp out Christianity. He was not blaming them for beating him; he would have done the same thing before.

5 The high priest and all the Council (the Sanhedrin) could themselves testify to the fact that Paul was a persecutor of Christians. If anyone had doubts about this, let him consult the high priest or any member of the Council. He even obtained letters from them to their associates in Damascus, and went there to bring these people as prisoners to Jerusalem to be punished.

Paul's Conversion

Verses 6-11: "About noon as I came near Damascus, suddenly a bright light from heaven flashed around me. ⁷ I fell to the ground and heard a voice say to me, 'Saul! Saul! Why do you persecute me?' ⁸ "'Who are you, Lord?' I asked." 'I am Jesus of Nazareth, whom you are persecuting,' he replied. ⁹ My companions saw the light, but they did not understand the voice of him who was speaking to me. ¹⁰ "'What shall I do, Lord?' I asked." 'Get up,' the Lord said, 'and go into Damascus. There you will be told all that you have been assigned to do.' ¹¹ My companions led me by the hand into Damascus, because the brilliance of the light had blinded me.

6 Luke records Paul's dramatic conversion three times in Acts: in Acts 9, here in Acts 22, and later in Acts 26. His conversion experience was a major turning point in church history. His conversion was not a matter of defection but of divine intervention.

Paul described what happened on his way to Damascus a few years prior to this. "About noon as I came near Damascus, suddenly a bright light from heaven flashed around me." Paul related what happened to him on his way to Damascus. At about noon, a bright light flashed around him and his companions.

7 Paul fell to the ground and heard a voice say to him, "Saul! Saul! Why do you persecute me?" Paul had been confronted by the Lord. It was fitting for the proud Pharisee to be thrown to the ground. He was temporarily blinded, confused, and scared. The voice asked why he kept persecuting Him. He did not understand what the question was for.

8 "Who are you, Lord?" Paul asked. "I am Jesus of Nazareth, whom you are persecuting," He replied. Jesus referred to Himself as "Jesus of Nazareth," a title which occurs seven times in Acts. In persecuting the Christians, Paul had been persecuting their Lord. Paul suddenly realized how terribly wrong he had been and that Jesus was alive. There and then, he exchanged Judaism for Jesus.

9 His companions saw the light, but they did not understand the voice of Him who was speaking to Paul. They stood speechless while Jesus was addressing Paul. They did not see the risen Jesus. "They saw the light, but did not see it as a revelation of Jesus in glory. They heard the voice, but only as a noise, and did not make out the words."[1]

10 "What shall I do, Lord?" he asked. "Get up," the Lord instructed, "and go into Damascus. There you will be told all that you have been assigned to do." A person like Paul who had seen the Lord wanted to serve Him by doing things according to the Lord's will. Jesus had a plan for Paul. The full scope of that plan was not revealed; only the first step was made known. Paul could not take the second step if he had not taken the first one. We discover God's plan for our lives by taking single steps of faith. "The just shall live by faith" (Romans 1:17, KJV).

11 "My companions led me by the hand into Damascus, because the brilliance of the light had blinded me." Paul was led by his companions into the city, where he would later meet Ananias. Paul reached his destination, not as the Lord's adversary but as an ally. He arrived blind; he had to depend on others to guide him. In blindness, Paul was left to think, pray, reflect, and reevaluate his whole life.

Paul's Sight was Restored

*Verses 12-16: "A man named Ananias came to see me. He was a devout observer of the law and highly respected by all the Jews living there. *¹³* He stood beside me and said, 'Brother Saul, receive your sight!' And at that very moment I was able to see him. *¹⁴* "Then he said: 'The God of our ancestors has chosen you to know his will and to see the Righteous One and to hear words from his mouth. *¹⁵* You will be his witness to all people of what you have seen and heard. *¹⁶* And now what are you waiting for? Get up, be baptized and wash your sins away, calling on his name.'*

12 Paul now described the role of Ananias in his conversion. A man named Ananias was sent by the Lord to see Paul in Damascus. He was a devout observer of the law and highly respected by all the Jews living there. Ananias was a man of impeccable character. His name was above reproach. It was this fellow Jew who introduced Paul to Christ.

13 Ananias not only introduced Paul to Christ, he was also instrumental in restoring his sight. He stood beside Paul and said, "Brother Saul, receive your sight!" And at that very moment he was able to see Ananias. God miraculously gave him back his sight. Ananias addressed Paul as a "brother," in spite of his being a former church persecutor. He accepted him as a fellow believer in Christ.

14 Paul quoted what Ananias said in part. Ananias said: "The God of our ancestors has chosen you to know his will and to see the Righteous One and to hear words from his mouth." The God of Abraham, Isaac, and Jacob had chosen Paul to know His will. He was also chosen to see the "Righteous One," title for the Messiah. We did not choose Christ; He chose us (John 15:16). God's sovereign selection of people for salvation does not absolve us of the responsibility to respond to His call properly.

15 Paul was called to be His witness to all people of what he had seen and heard. He became a first-hand witness of the fact that Jesus died, was resurrected and glorified. Paul, the former persecutor of Christians, had now become the main apologist for Christianity. He was commissioned by God to proclaim the gospel to all men. This would include the Jews and Gentiles.

16 "And now what are you waiting for? Get up, be baptized and wash your sins away, calling on his name." Paul was asked to act straightaway and get baptized. Baptism is an act of obedience that publicly identifies one with Christ. Although baptism follows salvation, it is not required for salvation. Baptism does not wash away sin; the blood of Jesus does that. Paul was born again before he was baptized.

Divine Command to Leave Jerusalem

Verses 17-21: "When I returned to Jerusalem and was praying at the temple, I fell into a trance [18] *and saw the Lord speaking to me. 'Quick!' he said. 'Leave Jerusalem immediately, because the people here will not accept your testimony about me.'* [19] *"'Lord,' I replied, 'these people know that I went from one synagogue to another to imprison and beat those who believe in you.* [20] *And when the blood of your martyr Stephen was shed, I stood there giving my approval and guarding the clothes of those who were killing him.'* [21] *"Then the Lord said to me, 'Go; I will send you far away to the Gentiles.'"*

17,18 After his conversion, scholars believe that Paul spent some time in Arabia, returned to Damascus, and paid a brief visit to Jerusalem. This was his first trip to Jerusalem after his conversion. "When I returned to Jerusalem and was praying at the temple, I fell into a trance and saw the Lord speaking to me. 'Quick!' he said. 'Leave Jerusalem immediately, because the people here will not accept your testimony about me.'" God speaks to His own people in different ways—through trances, visions, dreams, prophecy, godly advice, circumstances, etc. "His shocking turnabout, from Christian persecutor to Christian preacher, outraged the unbelieving Jews, who deemed him an apostate and blasphemer."[2] The Jews in Jerusalem were not ready to listen to Paul.

19,20 "'Lord,' I replied, 'these people know that I went from one synagogue to another to imprison and beat those who believe in you. And when the blood of your martyr Stephen was shed, I stood there giving my approval and guarding the clothes of those who were killing him.'" Paul related the persecutions he has brought to Christians. He confessed that he played a major role in the martyrdom of Stephen. He apparently felt that his audience would easily see what change had taken place in his life.

21 Paul resisted the need to leave Jerusalem. He was wrong to think that his drastic transformation would convince unbelieving Jews of the truth of the gospel. God knew better and did not argue with Paul. He simply ordered him to get out of Jerusalem. "Then the Lord said to me, 'Go; I will send you far away to the Gentiles.'" Jerusalem was not the main mission field for Paul. His mission field was primarily the Gentile world. By obeying the Lord and listening to some Christian advice, Paul saved his life.

NOTES

1. Howard I. Marshall, *Acts: Tyndale New Testament Commentaries* (Downers Grove, IL: InterVarsity Press, 1980), p. 375.
2. John MacArthur, *The MacArthur New Testament Commentary: Acts 13-28* (Chicago, IL: Moody Publishers, 1996), p. 270.

CHAPTER 22

PAUL, THE ROMAN CITIZEN

Acts 22:22-29

The Mob Rages Against Paul

Verses 22-24: The crowd listened to Paul until he said this. Then they raised their voices and shouted, "Rid the earth of him! He's not fit to live!" 23 As they were shouting and throwing off their cloaks and flinging dust into the air, 24 the commander ordered that Paul be taken into the barracks. He directed that he be flogged and interrogated in order to find out why the people were shouting at him like this.

22 The crowd listened to Paul until he mentioned that God sent him to the Gentiles. For Paul to go to the Gentiles was disgusting to them. It aroused their animosity and seemed so absurd that they would not hear him any longer. Then they raised their voices and shouted, "Rid the earth of him! He's not fit to live!" They yelled, screamed, and reviled Paul as unfit to live. They could have stoned Paul had the soldiers not been present.

23,24 As they were shouting and throwing off their cloaks and flinging dust into the air, the commander ordered that Paul be taken into the barracks. He directed that he be flogged and interrogated in order to find out why the people were shouting at him like this. They tore their outer garments and threw dust in the air as an indication of their anger. These actions also expressed their utter rejection of Paul and his message.

The commander, Claudius Lysias, realizing he was getting nowhere with the crowd, ordered Paul be taken to the barracks. His next plan of action would be to have Paul flogged and interrogate him concerning the source of the trouble. He believed that torturing Paul would cause him to confess. Remember Paul spoke to the crowd in Aramaic and the commander might not understand his defense. He was still ignorant of the real cause of the riot.

Paul Claims Roman Citizenship

Verses 25-29 : As they stretched him out to flog him, Paul said to the centurion standing there, "Is it legal for you to flog a Roman citizen who hasn't even been found guilty?" 26 When the centurion heard this, he went to the commander and reported it. "What are you going to do?" he asked. "This man is a Roman citizen." 27 The commander went to Paul and asked, "Tell me, are you a Roman citizen?" "Yes, I am," he answered. 28 Then the commander said, "I had to pay a lot of money for my citizenship." "But I was born a citizen," Paul replied. 29 Those who were about to interrogate him withdrew immediately. The commander himself was alarmed when he realized that he had put Paul, a Roman citizen, in chains.

25 As they stretched him out to flog him, Paul said to the centurion standing there, "Is it legal for you to flog a Roman citizen who hasn't even been found guilty?" He brought it to the attention of the centurion supervising his beating that they were violating his human rights as a Roman citizen. As long as we are not compromising our faith, it is proper to claim our civil rights and seek protection of the law. "To bind a Roman citizen was serious enough, but to scourge him was wholly illegal, and to do either to an uncondemned Roman was worst of all."[1]

26 When the centurion heard this, he went to the commander, his superior officer, and reported it. "What are you going to do?" he asked. "This man is a Roman citizen." He was warning the commander not to go any further. The news alarmed the commander, Lysias, fearing possible repercussions. A Roman citizen could not be whipped until a fair trial had been made.

27 The commander went to Paul at once and questioned Paul for himself. He asked directly, "Tell me, are you a Roman citizen?" "Yes, I am," he answered. The commander did not doubt Paul's claim because he knew that a false claim was punishable by death. He was subject to some penalty for even asking Paul to be flogged. Scholars have speculated on how Paul's family got their citizenship.

28 Then the commander said, "I had to pay a lot of money for my citizenship." "But I was born a citizen," Paul replied. Again, the commander had misjudged Paul. The Emperor Claudius had made Roman citizenship available to virtually everyone who could pay the large sum of money. Since the commander was named "Claudius" (Acts 23:26), it is safe to assume that he got his citizenship during the reign of the emperor.

29 Those who were about to interrogate him withdrew immediately. The commander himself was alarmed when he realized that he had put Paul, a Roman citizen, in chains without a hearing. Henceforth Lysias was kind to Paul now that he knew Paul was a Roman citizen. Paul was most likely freed from his chains but still remained in the barracks.

As John MacArthur rightly said, "Paul maintained the proper attitude—one of selfless love. It was his love for other believers that brought him to Jerusalem (to deliver the offering)… And it was his love for God that motivated his love for people and caused him to give glory to Him."[2]

NOTES

1. John Phillips, *Exploring Acts* (Grand Rapids, MI: Kregel Publications, 1986), p. 459.
2. John MacArthur, *The MacArthur New Testament Commentary: Acts 13-28* (Chicago, IL: Moody Publishers, 1996), p. 273.

CHAPTER 23

PAUL BEFORE THE SANHEDRIN

Acts 22:30-23:11

The Confrontation

Verses 22:30-23:5: ²²:³⁰ *The commander wanted to find out exactly why Paul was being accused by the Jews. So the next day he released him and ordered the chief priests and all the members of the Sanhedrin to assemble. Then he brought Paul and had him stand before them.* ²³:¹ *Paul looked straight at the Sanhedrin and said, "My brothers, I have fulfilled my duty to God in all good conscience to this day."* ² *At this the high priest Ananias ordered those standing near Paul to strike him on the mouth.* ³ *Then Paul said to him, "God will strike you, you whitewashed wall! You sit there to judge me according to the law, yet you yourself violate the law by commanding that I be struck!"* ⁴ *Those who were standing near Paul said, "How dare you insult God's high priest!"* ⁵ *Paul replied, "Brothers, I did not realize that he was the high priest; for it is written: 'Do not speak evil about the ruler of your people.'"*

22:30 The commander, Claudius Lysias, wanted to find out exactly why Paul was being accused by the Jews. Lysias realized the religious nature of what they were accusing Paul about, and sought help from the highest Jewish court. So the next day he released Paul and ordered the chief priests and all the members of the Sanhedrin to assemble. (The Sanhedrin consisted of about 70 to 72 men.) Then he brought Paul and had him stand before them. He probably assumed that the Sanhedrin would be unbiased in their judgment of Paul.

1 Paul looked straight at the Sanhedrin and said, "My brothers, I have fulfilled my duty to God in all good conscience to this day." He fixed his eyes intently on the council and addressed the Sanhedrin members as brothers, as equals. He was reminding them that he was one of them. He knew he had done nothing wrong. He had a good conscience which passed moral judgment on his actions. A conscience is the inner judge in us that declares what we do as right or wrong.

2 The high priest Ananias (should not be confused with Annas in Acts 4:6) was enraged by Paul's claim to have a good conscience all his life. He was the president of the council at that time. He ordered those standing near Paul to strike him on the mouth, as a way of silencing Paul. Ananias was known to have brought dishonor to the noble office. He himself was without good conscience. According to Howard Marshall, "He had been appointed c. AD 47, and was dismissed in AD 58-59. Later he was assassinated by a pro-Roman by Jewish guerrillas (AD 66)."[1]

3 Paul responded to the illegal command that Ananias gave. He was struck illegally without accusation or trial (Deuteronomy 25:2). He said to him, "God will strike you, you whitewashed wall! You sit there to judge me according to the law, yet you yourself violate the law by commanding that I be struck!" Paul's use of the word "whitewashed" was similar to how Jesus used it to describe the scribes and Pharisees (Matthew 23:27). He chastised the high priest without realizing who he was.

4 There was no attempt on the part of the rest of the Sanhedrin to challenge the action of the high priest. Some remained silent, while others rebuked Paul. Those who were standing near Paul said, "How dare you insult God's high priest!" The high priest occupied a position of authority and should be respected (Deuteronomy 17:8-12). To abuse him was tantamount to blasphemy.

5 Paul immediately admitted his fault and apologized. He replied, "Brothers, I did not realize that he was the high priest; for it is written: 'Do not speak evil about the ruler of your people.'" He quoted Exodus 22:28. Since the meeting was an informal gathering of the Sanhedrin, Ananias might not dress like a high priest and Paul might not recognize him as such. Paul's visit to Jerusalem over the past years had been sporadic and he might never have seen the high priest.

The Conquest

Verses 6-10: Then Paul, knowing that some of them were Sadducees and the others Pharisees, called out in the Sanhedrin, "My brothers, I am a Pharisee, descended from Pharisees. I stand on trial because of the hope of the resurrection of the dead." ⁷ When he said this, a dispute broke out between the Pharisees and the Sadducees, and the assembly was divided. ⁸ (The Sadducees say that there is no resurrection, and that there are neither angels nor spirits, but the Pharisees believe all these things.) ⁹ There was a great uproar, and some of the teachers of the law who were Pharisees stood up and argued vigorously. "We find nothing wrong with this man," they said. "What if a spirit or an angel has spoken to him?" ¹⁰ The dispute became so violent that the commander was afraid Paul would be torn to pieces by them. He ordered the troops to go down and take him away from them by force and bring him into the barracks.

6 After the confrontation between Paul and the high priest, Paul sensed he might not have a fair hearing from the Sanhedrin. Then Paul, knowing that some of them were Sadducees and the others Pharisees, called out to the Sanhedrin, "My brothers, I am a Pharisee, descended from Pharisees. I stand on trial because of the hope of the resurrection of the dead." Paul himself had been a Pharisee (Philippians 3:5). He realized that there is no Christianity without Jesus' resurrection.

7 Paul's tactic worked with immediate effect. His declaration of himself as a Pharisee split the council. With Paul aligning himself with the Pharisees, a dispute broke out between the Pharisees and the Sadducees, and the assembly was divided. Paul's appeal aroused the tensions between the two religious factions. They began to quarrel among themselves.

8 Luke briefly presents the distinctions between the two religious groups for the benefit of his readers who might not know. The Sadducees believed that there is no resurrection, and that there are neither angels nor spirits, but the Pharisees believed all these things. The Sadducees were the liberals, while Pharisees were the conservative fundamentalists. "It was much easier for a Pharisee to become a Christian than for a Sadducee, who denied miracles and the resurrection."[2]

9 There was a great uproar and confusion. Some of the teachers of the law who were Pharisees stood up and argued vigorously. They were ready to defend a fellow Pharisee. "We find nothing wrong with this man," they said. "What if a spirit or an angel has spoken to him?" The Pharisees were on Paul's side and demanded that the council acquit him. The Sadducees remained Paul's chief opponents.

10 The dispute became so violent that the commander was afraid Paul would be torn to pieces by them. He ordered the troops to go down and take him away from them by force and bring him into the barracks. Again, Paul had to be rescued from his own people by the soldiers. Paul's "crime" could not be determined in such a hostile atmosphere. Nothing more could be gained from the divided council.

The Consolation

Verse 11: The following night the Lord stood near Paul and said, "Take courage! As you have testified about me in Jerusalem, so you must also testify in Rome."

11 Paul was in the barracks reflecting on his situation. He did not know what would happen to him now. The devil might have whisped words of discouragement. The Lord has a way of silencing the enemy. The following night the Lord stood near Paul and said, "Take courage! As you have testified about me in Jerusalem, so you must also testify in Rome." Paul was not rebuked for going to Jerusalem. Rather, the Lord commended him for witnessing for Him there and encouraged him that he would do the same in Rome as he desired.

The Lord had spoken to Paul on at least two previous occasions (Acts 18:9; 22:17). This was a great relief and comfort to Paul. The Lord's promise sustained him through the several trials he endured. To know that the Lord is with us is a great source of encouragement.

NOTES

1. Howard I. Marshall, *Acts: Tyndale New Testament Commentaries* (Downers Grove, IL: InterVarsity Press, 1980), p. 382.
2. John Phillips, *Exploring Acts* (Grand Rapids, MI: Kregel Publications, 1986), p. 442.

CHAPTER 24

THE PLOT TO KILL PAUL

Acts 23:12-22

The Conspiracy

*Verses 12-15: The next morning some Jews formed a conspiracy and bound themselves with an oath not to eat or drink until they had killed Paul. *[13]* More than forty men were involved in this plot. *[14]* They went to the chief priests and the elders and said, "We have taken a solemn oath not to eat anything until we have killed Paul. *[15]* Now then, you and the Sanhedrin petition the commander to bring him before you on the pretext of wanting more accurate information about his case. We are ready to kill him before he gets here."*

12 Attempts on Paul's life by the Jews had been frustrated twice. The mob attempted lynching him, but the soldiers rescued Paul. His appearance before the Sanhedrin did not produce the desired result; they were unable to convict him of any wrongdoing. The next morning some Jews formed a conspiracy and bound themselves with an oath not to eat or drink until they had killed Paul. They were so sure and determined that they would get him this time around. Knowing from hindsight that these zealots did not succeed in their plan, they might have broken their oath or starved to death.

13 The plot against Paul was strong. It involved more than forty men. They realized that they could not depend on the Roman legal system to get rid of Paul because he had not committed any capital crime. So they decided to take action on their own. Caring less about their own lives, they were willing to face the Roman soldiers guarding Paul. They had forgotten that Paul was the servant of the exalted Lord, who was watching them. The Lord had assured Paul of safe passage to Rome. No weapon fashioned against Paul would prevail (Isaiah 54:17).

14 They went to the chief priests and the elders and said, "We have taken a solemn oath not to eat anything until we have killed Paul." The religious leaders took them in confidence and raised no protest. That says a lot about the spiritual leadership of Israel at that time. These men were without morals; they were easily persuaded to participate in this kind of illegal activity.

15 These Jews sought the full support and cooperation of the chief priests and the elders. They advised them on what to do on their part. "Now then, you and the Sanhedrin petition the commander to bring him before you on the pretext of wanting more accurate information about his case. We are ready to kill him before he gets here." Their plan was simple—just get Paul moved from the barracks to the council chamber under the guise of further examination; they would ambush and murder him on the way.

The Conspiracy is Discovered

Verses 16-22: But when the son of Paul's sister heard of this plot, he went into the barracks and told Paul. ¹⁷ Then Paul called one of the centurions and said, "Take this young man to the commander; he has something to tell him." ¹⁸ So he took him to the commander. The centurion said, "Paul, the prisoner, sent for me and asked me to bring this young man to you because he has something to tell you." ¹⁹ The commander took the young man by the hand, drew him aside and asked, "What is it you want to tell me?" ²⁰ He said: "Some Jews have agreed to ask you to bring Paul before the Sanhedrin tomorrow on the pretext of wanting more accurate information about him. ²¹ Don't give in to them, because more than forty of them are waiting in ambush for him. They have taken an oath not to eat or drink until they have killed him. They are ready now, waiting for your consent to their request." ²² The commander dismissed the young man with this warning: "Don't tell anyone that you have reported this to me."

16 It is easy for God to overthrow the plan of wicked men. With so many people involved in the conspiracy, it could not be kept confidential for too long. The son of Paul's sister heard of this plot; he went into the barracks and told Paul. We do not know much about Paul's family and exactly how Paul's nephew heard about the plot. When he stumbled across the information, he lost no time in bringing it to Paul's attention.

17 Although Paul was in custody, he was allowed to receive visitors. Paul called one of the centurions and said, "Take this young man to the commander; he has something to tell him." To avoid any dilution that might result in going through intermediaries, Paul wanted the commander to hear directly from his nephew. The centurion listened to Paul and delivered the message.

18 So he took Paul's nephew to the commander. The centurion said, "Paul, the prisoner, sent for me and asked me to bring this young man to you because he has something to tell you." He delivered Paul's message to the commander. The news spread from the young man to Paul, from Paul to the centurion, and from the centurion to the commander.

19 The commander took the young man by the hand. Since the matter appeared secret, he drew the boy aside and asked, "What is it you want to tell me?" It was easy for the commander to ignore the boy. But he was ready to listen to the boy. How would he know that the young man was telling the truth? The integrity and courage of the commander should be admired.

20 He said: "Some Jews have agreed to ask you to bring Paul before the Sanhedrin tomorrow on the pretext of wanting more accurate information about him." The boy repeated his story, which we already know. He gave the commander a detailed report about the plot. Some Jews were planning to take Paul's life the next day; the plotters would not want to fast for too long.

21 "Don't give in to them, because more than forty of them are waiting in ambush for him. They have taken an oath not to eat or drink until they have killed him. They are ready now, waiting for your consent to their request." The boy's language implies that the Jews were prepared, just waiting for the commander's consent. The boy urged the commander not to give in to the Jews.

22 The commander dismissed the young man with this warning: "Don't tell anyone that you have reported this to me." The commander knew about the plot before the Sanhedrin approached him. With a warning, he let the boy go. Secrecy was essential if the plot was to be avoided. If the Jews knew that he did not know about the plot, they could not suspect his intension for sending Paul to Caesarea.

CHAPTER 25

PAUL TRANSFERRED TO CAESAREA

Acts 23:23-35

Lysias Orders Two Centurions

Verses 23,24: Then he called two of his centurions and ordered them, "Get ready a detachment of two hundred soldiers, seventy horsemen and two hundred spearmen to go to Caesarea at nine tonight. [24] Provide horses for Paul so that he may be taken safely to Governor Felix."

23 The commander's immediate action indicates that he took the report seriously. He decided to get Paul out of Jerusalem as soon as possible. He called two of his centurions and ordered them, "Get ready a detachment of two hundred soldiers, seventy horsemen and two hundred spearmen to go to Caesarea at nine tonight." He had 470 men to protect Paul—200 soldiers, 200 spearmen, and 70 mounted troops. The men were to leave Jerusalem at 9pm and travel down to Caesarea, a sixty-mile journey. Caesarea was the Roman capital of Judea and the home of the Roman governor, Felix.

24 In addition to providing soldiers to protect Paul, the commander ordered that they provide horses for Paul so that he might be taken safely to Governor Felix, whose headquarters was in Caesarea He took no chances. He arranged 470 men to guard just one prisoner! He certainly gave Paul a royal treatment. "Caesar himself could not have been better protected."[1]

Lysias Writes Felix

Verses 25-30: He wrote a letter as follows: [26] *Claudius Lysias,*
To His Excellency, Governor Felix.
Greetings.

[27] *This man was seized by the Jews and they were about to kill him, but I came with my troops and rescued him, for I had learned that he is a Roman citizen.* [28] *I wanted to know why they were accusing him, so I brought him to their Sanhedrin.* [29] *I found that the accusation had to do with questions about their law, but there was no charge against him that deserved death or imprisonment.* [30] *When I was informed of a plot to be carried out against the man, I sent him to you at once. I also ordered his accusers to present to you their case against him.*

25,26 This is the only example of a secular letter in the NT. The purpose of the letter was to accompany Paul to the Roman governor Felix. The accompanying official letter would explain why Paul was sent. The commander wrote the letter as follows: Claudius Lysias, To His Excellency, Governor Felix. The commander's full name is Claudius Lysias, mentioned here for the first time. He addressed the letter to Governor Felix, his immediate superior. Felix was the governor of Judea from A.D. 52 to A.D. 59. The governor had his residence in Caesarea. His third wife was Drusilla, who was the daughter of Herod Agrippa I (Acts 24:24).

27 "This man was seized by the Jews and they were about to kill him, but I came with my troops and rescued him, for I had learned that he is a Roman citizen." The main body of the letter begins by mentioning how the commander intervened and rescued Paul from his would-be murderers. Lysias did not know that Paul was a Roman citizen until after he had chained Paul and ordered him to be flogged. He omitted this in his letter. Otherwise, the letter was fairly accurate.

28 "I wanted to know why they were accusing him, so I brought him to their Sanhedrin." The commander stated the matter in such a way that his official acts were commendable. In an effort to know what the real problem was, Lysias brought Paul before the Sanhedrin. Lysias intended to show that Paul had been tried by the Jewish religious Council. But the attempt to seek clarity from the Sanhedrin was fruitless.

29 "I found that the accusation had to do with questions about their law, but there was no charge against him that deserved death or imprisonment." He found that the accusation was related to their religious law. That was a theological matter, which held no real interest for the Romans. The commander gave his own opinion of Paul; he had done nothing worthy of death or imprisonment.

30 "When I was informed of a plot to be carried out against the man, I sent him to you at once. I also ordered his accusers to present to you their case against him." The commander portrayed himself as a champion of Roman justice and order. Those accusing Paul would have to go to Caesarea to make their case against him. The matter would be properly settled in Caesarea.

From Jerusalem to Caesarea

Verses 31-35: So the soldiers, carrying out their orders, took Paul with them during the night and brought him as far as Antipatris. ³² The next day they let the cavalry go on with him, while they returned to the barracks. ³³ When the cavalry arrived in Caesarea, they delivered the letter to the governor and handed Paul over to him. ³⁴ The governor read the letter and asked what province he was from. Learning that he was from Cilicia, ³⁵ he said, "I will hear your case when your accusers get here." Then he ordered that Paul be kept under guard in Herod's palace.

31 So the soldiers, carrying out their orders, took Paul with them during the night. Leaving at 9 pm, they brought him as far as Antipatris, which was about 40 miles from Jerusalem and 20 miles from Caesarea. Antipatris was rebuilt by Herod the Great, who also renamed it after his father, Antipater. The small town served as a rest stop for travelers. The troops spent the night there.

32 The next day they let the cavalry (the horsemen) go on with Paul, while the foot soldiers returned to the barracks in Jerusalem. In other words, the 200 soldiers and 200 spearmen returned to Jerusalem, while the 70 horsemen escorted Paul. Having passed the dangerous zone, Paul was now at a safe distance from Jerusalem and the cavalry escort was enough to take Paul safely to Caesarea.

33 When the cavalry arrived in Caesarea, they delivered the letter to the Governor Felix and handed Paul over to him. Paul was safe from the Jews plotting against his life. But was Paul safe from Felix? Felix was regarded as a cruel and greedy ruler. He held the same position that Pontius Pilate held during Jesus' time. The historian Tacitus described Felix as: "He exercised the power of a king with the mind of a slave."

34,35 The governor acted in a proper legal manner when Paul arrived. He read the letter and asked what province Paul was from. Felix wanted to know if he had the jurisdiction to try his case. The practice back then was to try criminals in the province where the crime was committed. Learning that Paul was from Cilicia, he said, "I will hear your case when your accusers get here." Then he ordered that Paul be kept under guard in Herod's palace. He was put in the guardroom attached to the palace built by Herod the Great rather than being housed in the common prison.

NOTES

1. John Phillips, *Exploring Acts* (Grand Rapids, MI: Kregel Publications, 1986), p. 447.

CHAPTER 26

PAUL BEFORE FELIX

Acts 24:1-21

Jewish Accusations

Verses 1-9: Five days later the high priest Ananias went down to Caesarea with some of the elders and a lawyer named Tertullus, and they brought their charges against Paul before the governor. ² When Paul was called in, Tertullus presented his case before Felix: "We have enjoyed a long period of peace under you, and your foresight has brought about reforms in this nation. ³ Everywhere and in every way, most excellent Felix, we acknowledge this with profound gratitude. ⁴ But in order not to weary you further, I would request that you be kind enough to hear us briefly. ⁵ "We have found this man to be a troublemaker, stirring up riots among the Jews all over the world. He is a ringleader of the Nazarene sect ⁶ and even tried to desecrate the temple; so we seized him. ⁸ By examining him yourself you will be able to learn the truth about all these charges we are bringing against him." ⁹ The other Jews joined in the accusation, asserting that these things were true.

1 Five days after Paul got to Caesarea, the accusers arrived from Jerusalem. They consisted of the high priest Ananias, some of the elders, and a lawyer named Tertullus. Lysias must have informed them that Paul had been sent to Caesarea. They brought their charges against Paul before the governor. They hired a high-powered attorney, Tertullus, an expert in Roman law, to formally present their case.

2-4 When Paul was called in, Tertullus spoke up on behalf of the Jews. He presented his case before Felix: "We have enjoyed a long period of peace under you, and your foresight has brought about reforms in this nation. Everywhere and in every way, most excellent Felix, we acknowledge this with profound gratitude. But in order not to weary you further, I would request that you be kind enough to hear us briefly."

The introductory part of Tertullus' speech was essentially flattering the governor. It was designed mainly to capture the governor's good will. Tertullus sounded like a politician who would tell any lie to get people to vote for him. Such seemingly complementary words constitute a form of bribery. From these words, one would regard Felix as a paragon of virtue. But Felix had been known to be cruel, unfair, and brutal. He was so violent and corrupt that the Jews hated him. The Jews were never grateful for anything he did. Nevertheless, Tertullus set a favorable tone for the remainder of his speech.

5 "We have found this man to be a troublemaker, stirring up riots among the Jews all over the world. He is a ringleader of the Nazarene sect." He brought three charges against Paul. First, he accused Paul of causing trouble and stirring riots among the Jews. Paul was charged of being a political menace. Second, Paul was the ringleader of the sect known as the Nazarenes. The term "Nazarenes" is used to describe the followers of Jesus, who grew up in Nazareth. It is a scornful way of referring to Christianity.

6 Third, Paul was accused of trying to desecrate the temple in Jerusalem, the center of Jewish piety. This was a capital crime. So he was seized by the Jews. This charge led to Paul's arrest. Although Paul was in temple, where he was arrested, he had not profaned the temple. It was only a rumor that Paul had brought a Gentile (Trophimus, a Gentile from Ephesus) into the temple area strictly reserved for the Jews.

7 Some manuscripts do not have this verse: "But the commander, Lysias, came and with the use of much force snatched him from our hands." (It appears in the footnote in NIV.) This is a half-truth, which is always more difficult to refute than a lie. The truth is that the Jews were beating Paul to death, and the Roman soldiers came to his rescue.

8 "By examining him yourself you will be able to learn the truth about all these charges we are bringing against him." Tertullus concluded his speech abruptly by asking for Felix's indulgence: let governor examine or question Paul and get the truth for himself. "Standard legal procedure would have included the judge interrogating the defendant publicly, as Tertullus invites Felix to do."[1]

9 The other Jews joined in supporting the accusation, asserting that these things were true. The phrase "the other Jews" implies that Tertullus was a Jew. Tertullus' oratory was cheered by those who hired him. The other Jews merely echoed what their spokesman just said. One wonders how they expected to press their charges with false accusations.

Paul's Defense

Verses 10-21: When the governor motioned for him to speak, Paul replied: "I know that for a number of years you have been a judge over this nation; so I gladly make my defense. ¹¹ You can easily verify that no more than twelve days ago I went up to Jerusalem to worship. ¹² My accusers did not find me arguing with anyone at the temple, or stirring up a crowd in the synagogues or anywhere else in the city. ¹³ And they cannot prove to you the charges they are now making against me. ¹⁴ However, I admit that I worship the God of our ancestors as a follower of the Way, which they call a sect. I believe everything that is in accordance with the Law and that is written in the Prophets, ¹⁵ and I have the same hope in God as these men themselves have, that there will be a resurrection of both the righteous and the wicked. ¹⁶ So I strive always to keep my conscience clear before God and man. ¹⁷ "After an absence of several years, I came to Jerusalem to bring my people gifts for the poor and to present offerings. ¹⁸ I was ceremonially clean when they found me in the temple courts doing this. There was no crowd with me, nor was I involved in any disturbance. ¹⁹ But there are some Jews from the province of Asia, who ought to be here before you and bring charges if they have anything against me. ²⁰ Or these who are here should state what crime they found in me when I stood before the Sanhedrin— ²¹ unless it was this one thing I shouted as I stood in their presence: 'It is concerning the resurrection of the dead that I am on trial before you today.'"

10 Under the Roman law, one had the right to face his accusers and defend himself. The governor motioned for Paul to speak. Without a lawyer to represent him, He replied: "I know that for a number of years you have been a judge over this nation, so I gladly make my defense." Although Paul did not flatter Felix as Tertullus did, he did complement the judge. Felix had been judge over Palestine long enough to know the customs of the Jews. In other words, Paul acknowledged the fact that someone who was familiar with Jewish customs was judging the matter.

11 Paul started his defense by answering the charge of treason. "You can easily verify that no more than twelve days ago I went up to Jerusalem to worship." The short time Paul had spent in Jerusalem was not enough to cause an uprising. His goal for coming to Jerusalem was to worship as a visitor, not to incite a revolt. In fact, he was in Jerusalem basically to bring an offering for the poor. This fact could be verified by Governor Felix.

12 "My accusers did not find me arguing with anyone at the temple, or stirring up a crowd in the synagogues or anywhere else in the city." He did not address a crowd in the temple or stir up a crowd in the synagogues in Jerusalem. Even if he did, there was no crime in that. He was offering a sacrifice, not committing sacrilege. They could not prove any of their accusations.

13 "And they cannot prove to you the charges they are now making against me." The Sanhedrin could not prove the charges made against Paul. They had no evidence to support the charges. Their accusations were contrary to well-known facts. Virtually anyone could make accusations, but without proof, the accusations are false. Paul had been falsely accused and they had no proof.

14 "However, I admit that I worship the God of our ancestors as a follower of the Way, which they call a sect. I believe everything that is in accordance with the Law and that is written in the Prophets." Tertullus, the hired attorney, had described Christianity as the sect of the Nazarenes, but Paul called it the Way. He admitted that he was a worshiper of the God of our ancestors and the follower of Jesus, the Way. He was not ashamed to identify himself as a Christian. If anyone was to be accused of abandoning orthodoxy, it was Ananias and the Sadducees.

In fact, he was more orthodox than the Jews accusing Him. He believed in the Law and the Prophets and obeyed them.

15 "I have the same hope in God as these men themselves have, that there will be a resurrection of both the righteous and the wicked." Although the Sadducees did not believe in the resurrection, Paul declared his firm belief in it. The resurrection is the fundamental truth of the gospel. Everyone will be resurrected—the righteous will live in the eternal kingdom of God, while the unrighteous will live in eternal torment (Daniel 12:2).

16 Paul's belief was not limited to just mental assent. He strove always to keep his conscience clear before God and man. This was his rule of life. He made a similar statement when he stood before the Sanhedrin (Acts 23:1) several days before the speech was made. Our conscience is our moral compass and we should understand its role in providing guidance. As an upright man, Paul was guided by integrity (Proverbs 11:3). To the best of his ability, he tried to keep God's law and man's law.

17 After an absence of several years, Paul came to Jerusalem to bring his people gifts for the poor and to present offerings. He had collected a large offering from the Gentile believers for the church in Jerusalem. He came back to Jerusalem for the purpose of showing mercy to the poor. He also wanted to worship at the temple and offer offerings. This did not sound like a man causing trouble but a man who loved God and people. "Paul has shifted the focus of the proceedings from political charges to theological matters."[2]

18 "I was ceremonially clean when they found me in the temple courts doing this. There was no crowd with me, nor was I involved in any disturbance." Before Paul was arrested, he had already gone through the purification rites. Tertullus the attorney and Ananias the high priest were not there when the riot began. Their charges were based on hearsay, which was unacceptable as evidence in the Roman court.

19 "But there are some Jews from the province of Asia, who ought to be here before you and bring charges if they have anything against me." Those Asian Jews who falsely accused Paul should have been around to present their charges before Felix. Their absence indicates that they had nothing to substantiate their charges. They were good at causing riots, but not good at producing evidence.

20,21 "Or these who are here should state what crime they found in me when I stood before the Sanhedrin unless it was this one thing I shouted as I stood in their presence: 'It is concerning the resurrection of the dead that I am on trial before you today.'" There was no indication of Paul doing anything wrong and no uproar had been caused.

The only thing they could charge him for was that he stated his hope in the resurrection of the dead. Was it a crime to believe in the resurrection? Even some orthodox Jews believed in that. Although the resurrection of the dead was a controversial issue to the Jews, it was a non-issue to the Romans.

Thus, Paul had cleverly presented his case before Felix. He had refuted the charges made by Tertullus. Tertullus and the other Jews had no case at all. It was now Felix's turn to respond.

NOTES

1. Richard P. Thompson, *Acts: A Commentary in the Wesleyan Tradition* (Kansas City, KS: Beacon Hill Press, 2015), p. 378.
2. Ibid., p. 380.

CHAPTER 27

FELIX POSTPONES MAKING A DECISION

Acts 24:22-27

Paul's Case is Deferred

*Verses 22,23: Then Felix, who was well acquainted with the Way, adjourned the proceedings. "When Lysias the commander comes," he said, "I will decide your case." *²³* He ordered the centurion to keep Paul under guard but to give him some freedom and permit his friends to take care of his needs.*

22 Then Felix, who was well acquainted with the Way, adjourned the proceedings. He had been the governor for six years. He understood the Way to be Christianity. This understanding possibly came from his wife, Drusilla, who was Jewish. He knew that Christians were peace-lovers and law-abiding people, not political activists. He also knew that the charges against Paul were worthless. He faced a difficult situation. He decided not to make a decision at this time. He would wait till he could get more information from the commander. "When Lysias the commander comes," he said, "I will decide your case." So the Jews went back to Jerusalem without a decision or achieving their goal.

23 He ordered the centurion to keep Paul under guard but to give him some freedom and permit his friends to take care of his needs. Paul was kept in custody, but not kept in close confinement. He was given "free custody." That means that his friends could visit and care for him. We recall that Philip and his four daughters lived in Caesarea and might visit Paul. So was the church of Christ in the city.

The Second Hearing before Felix

Verses 24,25: Several days later Felix came with his wife Drusilla, who was Jewish. He sent for Paul and listened to him as he spoke about faith in Christ Jesus. ²⁵ As Paul talked about righteousness, self-control and the judgment to come, Felix was afraid and said, "That's enough for now! You may leave. When I find it convenient, I will send for you."

24 Several days later Felix came with his wife Drusilla, who was Jewish. Drusilla was the youngest daughter of Herod Agrippa I. It was possible through her that Felix learned about the Way. Felix sent for Paul, his pet prisoner, and listened to him as he spoke about faith in Christ Jesus. Felix already knew about Christianity (v. 22). He probably just wanted to know more from Paul.

25 Paul talked about righteousness, self-control and the judgment to come. Paul addressed three keys issues in Christianity Felix should know. First, righteousness is living by God's standard. In other words, it is the divine standard by which human conduct is examined. Second, self-control is a character trait that puts ourselves in check. It is getting more and more difficult to control ourselves. We must exercise self-control in every area of our lives. Third, judgment indicates that God would hold humans accountable for the resources entrusted to them. God will judge our deeds through His Son whom He has appointed as the Judge (John 5:22,27). Judgment begins with God's family and ends with the ungodly.

Apparently Paul's sermon toughened Felix's conscience. Felix was afraid perhaps because of his immorality in relation to his third wife, Drusilla. He said, "That's enough for now! You may leave. When I find it convenient, I will send for you." When presented with the gospel, he postponed again. He was looking for a more convenient time to repent. Delaying salvation is dangerous (2 Corinthians 6:2; Isaiah 55:6). As they say, "Procrastination is the thief of time."

Paul was Imprisoned for Two Years

Verses 26,27: At the same time he was hoping that Paul would offer him a bribe, so he sent for him frequently and talked with him. [27] When two years had passed, Felix was succeeded by Porcius Festus, but because Felix wanted to grant a favor to the Jews, he left Paul in prison.

26 At the same time he was hoping that Paul would offer him a bribe, so he sent for him frequently and talked with him. It was apparently Felix's greed that kept Paul in prison for two years. But giving a bribe or receiving one was strictly prohibited by the Roman law. How much money could a prisoner have to give? Felix must have heard Paul talk about the financial gift he brought to Jerusalem to help the needy. To Felix, Paul was not a prisoner without means. In good conscience, Paul could not give him a bribe.

27 Time rolled by quickly. When two years had passed, Felix was toying with Paul. He was succeeded by Porcius Festus. Paul was innocent. With a lack of evidence to substantiate the charges, Felix should have had the courage to release Paul. But because Felix wanted to grant a favor to the Jews, he left Paul in prison. He probably had received a bribe from the Jews. When Festus resumed his office, he inherited the prisoner Paul.

CHAPTER 28

PAUL BEFORE FESTUS

Acts 25:1-12

The Hearing before Festus

Verses 1-7: Three days after arriving in the province, Festus went up from Caesarea to Jerusalem, ² where the chief priests and the Jewish leaders appeared before him and presented the charges against Paul. ³ They requested Festus, as a favor to them, to have Paul transferred to Jerusalem, for they were preparing an ambush to kill him along the way. ⁴ Festus answered, "Paul is being held at Caesarea, and I myself am going there soon. ⁵ Let some of your leaders come with me, and if the man has done anything wrong, they can press charges against him there." ⁶ After spending eight or ten days with them, Festus went down to Caesarea. The next day he convened the court and ordered that Paul be brought before him. ⁷ When Paul came in, the Jews who had come down from Jerusalem stood around him. They brought many serious charges against him, but they could not prove them.

1 The new governor Porcius Festus who succeeded Felix (Acts 24:27) reigned only for two years. He was regarded as a good governor during that short reign. He was a man of action. He wasted no time in visiting the Holy City. Three days after arriving in the province of Judea, Festus went up from Caesarea to Jerusalem. The purpose of the visit was probably to meet with the Jewish leaders and get familiar with them. Festus realized that maintaining peace in Judea depended largely on the leaders there.

2 In Jerusalem, the chief priests and the Jewish leaders appeared before Festus and presented the charges against Paul. The old high priest Ananias had died; he was now being replaced by Ishamel. Although Paul had been in prison in Caesarea for some two years, the Jewish leaders did not forget him. He was still on their mind. They wanted to seize this opportunity to get rid of Paul.

3 The fact that the Jewish leaders brought up Paul's case right away indicates how pressing the case was to them. They still regarded Paul as their bitter enemy and wanted him dead. They requested that Festus, as a favor to them, have Paul transferred to Jerusalem, for they were preparing an another ambush to kill him along the way. They reasoned that Paul's offense was religious rather than political; Paul would be better tried by the Sanhedrin in Jerusalem. If Paul was released by Festus, he might not get to Jerusalem alive.

4,5 Festus answered, "Paul is being held at Caesarea, and I myself am going there soon. Let some of your leaders come with me, and if the man has done anything wrong, they can press charges against him there." Transferring Paul from Caesarea to Jerusalem did not sound right to Festus. He could not see how Paul's case should be transfered to a lower court. So he did not grant their selfish request or yield to their manipulation. Rather he suggested that some of the leaders should follow him to Caesarea and press their charges against Paul there. God providentially used Festus to protect Paul from another plot against his life by his own people.

6 After spending eight or ten days with the people in Jerusalem, Festus went down to Caesarea. As a man of action, Festus convened the court the next day and ordered that Paul be brought before him. Paul's case had to be reopened. He had to go through the hassle of another trial. Since Roman law was on Paul's side, he could not be found guilty of any offense.

7 When Paul came in, the Jews who had come down from Jerusalem stood around him. They brought many serious charges against him, but they could not prove them. They could not back up any of them with proof. For two years, they still lacked witnesses or evidence to support their charges. Luke does not specify what the charges were, but Paul's defense shows that he was accused of disobeying the Jewish law, defiling the temple, and offending the Roman government (v. 8).

Paul Appeals to Caesar

Verses 8-12: Then Paul made his defense: "I have done nothing wrong against the Jewish law or against the temple or against Caesar." ⁹ Festus, wishing to do the Jews a favor, said to Paul, "Are you willing to go up to Jerusalem and stand trial before me there on these charges?" ¹⁰ Paul answered: "I am now standing before Caesar's court, where I ought to be tried. I have not done any wrong to the Jews, as you yourself know very well. ¹¹ If, however, I am guilty of doing anything deserving death, I do not refuse to die. But if the charges brought against me by these Jews are not true, no one has the right to hand me over to them. I appeal to Caesar!" ¹² After Festus had conferred with his council, he declared: "You have appealed to Caesar. To Caesar you will go!"

8 Paul was given the opportunity to defend himself. So Paul made his defense: "I have done nothing wrong against the Jewish law or against the temple or against Emperor Caesar." This statement is a summary of Paul's defense. He denied all the charges brought against him. He was innocent. God forbids bearing false charges against someone (Exodus 20:16). "He [Paul] declared simply that he had done nothing against the specifics of the law, the sanctity of the Temple, or the sovereignty of the emperor."[1]

9 Festus could not get much of these accusations and denials. He saw that no progress was made in Paul's trial. However, wishing to do the Jews a favor, he said to Paul, "Are you willing to go up to Jerusalem and stand trial before me there on these charges?" Festus mentioned that Paul's trial in Jerusalem would still be before him. Paul knew the Jewish leaders better than Festus. Returning to Jerusalem was going backward and it might mean death to Paul.

10 Paul answered: "I am now standing before Caesar's court, where I ought to be tried. I have not done any wrong to the Jews, as you yourself know very well." Paul knew he could never get a fair trial in Jerusalem. He was being held by the Roman authority and ought to be tried by the Roman law. Festus definitely had misjudged the apostle. He had forgotten that Paul was not just a Jew, but also a Roman citizen.

11 "If, however, I am guilty of doing anything deserving death, I do not refuse to die. But if the charges brought against me by these Jews are not true, no one has the right to hand me over to them. I appeal to Caesar!" Paul was not afraid of dying if he had done something deserving death.

A Roman citizen could directly appeal to Caesar if he felt justice was being denied to him. Paul exercised his right as a Roman citizen and appealed to Caesar. This would be like appealing to the Supreme Court today. If the appeal was granted, Paul's case would be transferred to the emperor in Rome. This did not mean that Caesar would personally hear the case but the case would be tried by the highest court in the Roman Empire. The Caesar in question here was Nero, whose reign started peacefully but quickly degenerated into violent behavior that led to his suicide.

12 To make sure he was taking the right step, Festus took counsel. After Festus had conferred with his council, he declared: "You have appealed to Caesar. To Caesar you will go!" Festus must have felt relieved that the difficult case had been taken out of his hands. Paul had desired to go to Rome and God had assured him that he would be there to testify of Him (Acts 23:11).

NOTES

1. John Phillips, *Exploring Acts* (Grand Rapids, MI: Kregel Publications, 1986), p. 464.

CHAPTER 29

PAUL BEFORE AGRIPPA – PART 1

Acts 25:13-27

Festus Informs Agrippa about Paul

Verses 13-22: A few days later King Agrippa and Bernice arrived at Caesarea to pay their respects to Festus. ¹⁴ Since they were spending many days there, Festus discussed Paul's case with the king. He said: "There is a man here whom Felix left us a prisoner. ¹⁵ When I went to Jerusalem, the chief priests and the elders of the Jews brought charges against him and asked that he be condemned. ¹⁶ "I told them that it is not the Roman custom to hand over anyone before they have faced their accusers and have had an opportunity to defend themselves against the charges. ¹⁷ When they came here with me, I did not delay the case, but convened the court the next day and ordered the man to be brought in. ¹⁸ When his accusers got up to speak, they did not charge him with any of the crimes I had expected. ¹⁹ Instead, they had some points of dispute with him about their own religion and about a dead man named Jesus who Paul claimed was alive. ²⁰ I was at a loss how to investigate such matters; so I asked if he would be willing to go to Jerusalem and stand trial there on these charges. ²¹ But when Paul made his appeal to be held over for the Emperor's decision, I ordered him held until I could send him to Caesar." ²² Then Agrippa said to Festus, "I would like to hear this man myself." He replied, "Tomorrow you will hear him."

13 As the governor, Festus was supposed to write a report and send it along with Paul to Rome. But since he did not understand the charges brought against Paul, it was difficult for him to write a good, coherent

153

report, detailing the charges. Help came through King Agrippa II. A few days after Paul appealed to Caesar, King Agrippa and Bernice arrived at Caesarea to pay their respects to Festus.

Agrippa and Bernice were actually brother and sister living together, in an incestuous relationship, which the Bible is against (Leviticus 18:9, Deuteronomy 27:22). Agrippa was the king over the Jews back then. Although Agrippa was Idumean, he practiced the Jewish religion and knew the Jewish Scriptures. He was the son of Agrippa I, the Herod that murdered James and arrested Peter.

14 Since they were spending many days there, that gave Festus an opportunity to seek the advice of King Agrippa on how he might handle Paul's situation. Festus discussed Paul's case with the king. Apparently, he related the story from his own point of view. He said: "There is a man here whom Felix left as a prisoner." It is true that Festus inherited this case from Felix.

15 "When I went to Jerusalem, the chief priests and the elders of the Jews brought charges against him and asked that he be condemned." The Jewish leaders did not want a fair trial for Paul. They just wanted him condemned. Festus added and omitted certain details in relating Paul's case to Agrippa. He did not mention the plot made against Paul.

16 "I told them that it is not the Roman custom to hand over anyone before they have faced their accusers and have had an opportunity to defend themselves against the charges." Festus did not hesitate to tell them what the Roman law required. The law does not convict a man before his trial. Festus did not grant their request. Paul had a right to present his own side of the story.

17 "When they came here with me, I did not delay the case, but convened the court the next day and ordered the man to be brought in." When the Jewish leaders came to Caesarea with Festus, he wasted no time in letting the prisoner be brought into his court. Festus gave a somewhat accurate report. His version of Paul's case placed him in a favorable light before Agrippa.

18 When his accusers got up to speak, they did not charge him with any of the crimes I had expected. Festus was disappointed that Paul's accusers could not come up with wrongdoing. He expected their charges would involve violations of the Roman law. None of their charges warranted Paul's imprisonment, let alone his death.

19 Instead, the religious leaders had some points of dispute with Paul about their own religion and about a dead man named Jesus, whom Paul claimed was alive. That was the crux of the matter. "Yet it was precisely the issue of the resurrection of Jesus Christ that most clearly set Christianity apart from Judaism and was the cornerstone of the gospel."[1] No mention was made of Paul defiling the temple or being a threat to public order.

20 "I was at a loss how to investigate such matters; so I asked if he would be willing to go to Jerusalem and stand trial there on these charges." Festus understood that it was basically a matter of religious questions, which he could not handle. "If Festus had trouble explaining matters to Caesar, how much more trouble he will have explaining things to God."[2]

21 "But when Paul made his appeal to be held over for the Emperor's decision, I ordered him held until I could send him to Caesar." Paul was not only seeking Roman justice, he was also appealing for Roman protection. Paul was kept in prison until he could be taken to Rome. God allowed Paul to be kept in Roman custody to protect him from assassination.

22 Then Agrippa said to Festus, "I would like to hear this man myself." Festus replied, "Tomorrow you will hear him." Festus was willing to convene another court hearing the next day. Although Agrippa trusted and believed Festus' report about Paul's trial, he still wanted to know more about it by directly hearing from Paul. Agrippa was eager and curious to see and hear Paul. His visit had been timely.

Festus Introduces Paul to the Assembly

Verses 23-27: The next day Agrippa and Bernice came with great pomp and entered the audience room with the high-ranking military officers and the

prominent men of the city. At the command of Festus, Paul was brought in.
²⁴ Festus said: "King Agrippa, and all who are present with us, you see this
man! The whole Jewish community has petitioned me about him in Jerusalem
and here in Caesarea, shouting that he ought not to live any longer. ²⁵ I found
he had done nothing deserving of death, but because he made his appeal to
the Emperor I decided to send him to Rome. ²⁶ But I have nothing definite
to write to His Majesty about him. Therefore I have brought him before all
of you, and especially before you, King Agrippa, so that as a result of this
investigation I may have something to write. ²⁷ For I think it is unreasonable
to send a prisoner on to Rome without specifying the charges against him."

23 The next day Agrippa and Bernice came with great pomp and
entered the audience room with the high-ranking military officers and
the prominent men of the city. A guard of soldiers escorted Agrippa,
Bernice, and prominent men of Caesarea wearing the finest clothes into
the auditorium. They were all assembled to hear Paul's defense. At the
command of Festus, Paul was brought in, shackled in chain. The real
royalty in the room was the controversial prisoner, the child of the Living
God, the King of kings.

24 Festus said: "King Agrippa, and all who are present with us, you
see this man! The whole Jewish community has petitioned me about
him in Jerusalem and here in Caesarea, shouting that he ought not
to live any longer." Festus began his introduction of Paul as a way of
opening the proceedings. The Jewish community wanted Paul dead.
Festus was exaggerating when he said "the whole Jewish community" in
Jerusalem and Caesarea had petitioned him. He was only referring to the
Sanhedrin, possibly as representing the nation.

25 In spite of the petition of the Jewish community, Festus found out
that Paul had done nothing deserving of death. Paul was innocent of any
charge. He lived a life of integrity. He had nothing to hide. His enemies
could not find any irregularities or inconsistencies in his life. But because
he made his appeal to the Emperor, Festus had decided that he would
send him to Rome.

26 "But I have nothing definite to write to His Majesty about him.
Therefore I have brought him before all of you, and especially before

you, King Agrippa, so that as a result of this investigation I may have something to write." Festus explained that the hearing was not a formal trial. His purpose of convening the court (or this regal assembly) was to be able to find something to write to the emperor about Paul. He wanted them to listen to Paul's story and come up with some charges he could write against him. What Festus really lacked was not charges against Paul, but evidence to substantiate them.

27 "For I think it is unreasonable to send a prisoner on to Rome without specifying the charges against him." To send a frivolous case like this to Caesar (Nero, A.D. 54-68) without stating the charges did not speak well of Festus. It would no reflect well on his competence and sound ridiculous. He hoped that as a result of this assembly Agrippa and other dignitaries could help him

NOTES

1. John MacArthur, *The MacArthur New Testament Commentary: Acts 13-28* (Chicago, IL: Moody Publishers, 1996), p. 328
2. John Phillips, *Exploring Acts* (Grand Rapids, MI: Kregel Publications, 1986), p. 469.

CHAPTER 30

PAUL BEFORE AGRIPPA – PART 2

Acts 26:1-23

Paul's Defense

Verses 1-3: Then Agrippa said to Paul, "You have permission to speak for yourself." So Paul motioned with his hand and began his defense: ² "King Agrippa, I consider myself fortunate to stand before you today as I make my defense against all the accusations of the Jews, ³ and especially so because you are well acquainted with all the Jewish customs and controversies. Therefore, I beg you to listen to me patiently.

1 Agrippa was in charge. Having listened to Governor Festus' opening comments, Agrippa said to Paul, "You have permission to speak for yourself." So Paul motioned with his hand and began his defense. This is Paul's last and longest defense in Acts. Since Agrippa was the key guest, Paul directed his address to him. His accusers were absent. So Paul did not mention the specific charges.

2,3 "King Agrippa, I consider myself fortunate to stand before you today as I make my defense against all the accusations of the Jews, and especially so because you are well acquainted with all the Jewish customs and controversies. Therefore, I beg you to listen to me patiently." Paul was fortunate to be standing before a man who was well versed in Jewish law and custom. Agrippa would have a better chance of understanding the truth about Jesus Christ than Festus. He seemed to stand in two worlds (Jewish and Roman) and represented both well. Knowing that he was prepared to tell the whole story, he asked for patience on the part of Agrippa and the other guests.

Paul's Background as a Pharisee

Verses 4-8: "The Jewish people all know the way I have lived ever since I was a child, from the beginning of my life in my own country, and also in Jerusalem. ⁵ They have known me for a long time and can testify, if they are willing, that I conformed to the strictest sect of our religion, living as a Pharisee. ⁶ And now it is because of my hope in what God has promised our ancestors that I am on trial today. ⁷ This is the promise our twelve tribes are hoping to see fulfilled as they earnestly serve God day and night. King Agrippa, it is because of this hope that these Jews are accusing me. ⁸ Why should any of you consider it incredible that God raises the dead?

4 "The Jewish people all know the way I have lived ever since I was a child, from the beginning of my life in my own country, and also in Jerusalem." Paul's defense was autobiographical in nature. It described Paul's early life and his Jewish heritage. The Jews knew about him, how he grew up in Tarsus and was educated under Gamaliel in Jerusalem (Acts 22:3). The young Saul of Tarsus made a name for himself. He was known for his scholarship, righteousness, and religious zeal.

5 They have known Paul for a long time and can testify, if they are willing, that he conformed to the strictest sect of their religion, living as a Pharisee (Philippians 3:5). His life was an open book that everyone in Jerusalem knew. Everyone knew Paul to be a devout Pharisee and the son of a Pharisee (Acts 23:6). The Pharisees seemed to belong to the most religious sect in Judaism and they interpreted the laws more accurately than others. Without a doubt, Paul was serious and zealous in his pursuit of Judaism.

6,7 "And now it is because of my hope in what God has promised our ancestors that I am on trial today. This is the promise our twelve tribes are hoping to see fulfilled as they earnestly serve God day and night. King Agrippa, it is because of this hope that these Jews are accusing me." The hope had to do with the coming of the Messiah and the resurrection related to that coming. Their ancestors all shared the same hope. Every godly woman in Israel had hoped to be the mother of the Messiah. Paul proclaimed that that the hope of Israel had come in the person of Jesus Christ. He was being accused for this proclamation. He was now a prisoner because of the hope of Israel.

Notice that Paul mentioned the twelve tribes. This sounded contrary to the theory that the ten northern tribes were mixed with other people and lost. God knows where His people are and will fulfill His promise to them.

8 Paul went on to say, "Why should any of you consider it incredible that God raises the dead?" God is sovereign and can do whatever He chooses to do. The God who created the whole universe and all within it can certainly raise the dead. He raised Jesus from the dead to demonstrate that He was the Messiah. If there were no resurrection, the faith of Abraham, Isaac, and Jacob would be meaningless.

Paul as a Persecutor

Verses 9-11: "I too was convinced that I ought to do all that was possible to oppose the name of Jesus of Nazareth. [10] And that is just what I did in Jerusalem. On the authority of the chief priests I put many of the Lord's people in prison, and when they were put to death, I cast my vote against them. [11] Many a time I went from one synagogue to another to have them punished, and I tried to force them to blaspheme. I was so obsessed with persecuting them that I even hunted them down in foreign cities.

9 In his defense, Paul briefly addressed his persecution of the Christians. "I too was convinced that I ought to do all that was possible to oppose the name of Jesus of Nazareth." Paul's zeal for Judaism led him to oppose the Way. He had intense hatred for the name of Jesus of Nazareth. This is the seventh and the last mention of "Jesus of Nazareth" in the book of Acts. The name had been obnoxious to Paul and he did everything to oppose it. He was on a one-man mission to wipe out anyone who had faith in Jesus Christ.

10 "And that is just what I did in Jerusalem. On the authority of the chief priests I put many of the Lord's people in prison, and when they were put to death, I cast my vote against them." Paul was armed with authority to stamp out Christianity. He saw it as his solemn duty to oppose the name of Jesus. He thought he could exterminate Christianity completely from the face of the earth. He was present when Stephen was stoned to death (Acts 7:58).

11 "Many a time I went from one synagogue to another to have them punished, and I tried to force them to blaspheme. I was so obsessed with persecuting them that I even hunted them down in foreign cities." Paul saw Christians as blasphemous heretics and he punished them as such. He pursued them from one synagogue to another. In the early days, most Christians were Jews and the synagogue was still their place of worship. Paul would go to the synagogues and force Christians to blaspheme.

Paul's Conversion and Commission

Verses 12-18: "On one of these journeys I was going to Damascus with the authority and commission of the chief priests. ¹³ About noon, King Agrippa, as I was on the road, I saw a light from heaven, brighter than the sun, blazing around me and my companions. ¹⁴ We all fell to the ground, and I heard a voice saying to me in Aramaic, 'Saul, Saul, why do you persecute me? It is hard for you to kick against the goads.' ¹⁵ "Then I asked, 'Who are you, Lord?' "'I am Jesus, whom you are persecuting,' the Lord replied. ¹⁶ 'Now get up and stand on your feet. I have appeared to you to appoint you as a servant and as a witness of what you have seen and will see of me. ¹⁷ I will rescue you from your own people and from the Gentiles. I am sending you to them ¹⁸ to open their eyes and turn them from darkness to light, and from the power of Satan to God, so that they may receive forgiveness of sins and a place among those who are sanctified by faith in me.'

12 In his defense, Paul now discussed his conversion experience. "On one of these journeys I was going to Damascus with the authority and commission of the chief priests." Paul was not satisfied with just persecuting Christians in Jerusalem. He pursued and persecuted them in other cities. On one occasion, he was journeying to Damascus with the authority and commission of the chief priests to persecute Christians there. He was to arrest as many Christians as possible and bring them to Jerusalem for punishment.

13 "About noon, King Agrippa, as I was on the road, I saw a light from heaven, brighter than the sun, blazing around me and my companions." The urgency of Paul's mission to Damascus forced him to travel in the mid-day heat rather than waiting for the cooler part of the day. "The sun at its brightest was outshone by the light of Christ's glory. The fact that it was mid-day made it easy to compare Christ's glory with the sun's brightest light."[1] The dazzling light made Paul and his companions fall down. The light was the glory of God.

14 "We all fell to the ground, and I heard a voice saying to me in Aramaic, 'Saul, Saul, why do you persecute me? It is hard for you to kick against the goads.'" Without realizing it, Saul had been rebellious. He has been kicking against the goads. "To fight God, as Saul was doing, was to fight a losing battle. It was as stupid as an ox kicking against the goads (sharpened rods used to herd cattle)."[2] Now Jesus spoke to him in Aramaic, his native tongue, and made him realize that he had been persecuting Him.

15 "Then I asked, 'Who are you, Lord?' 'I am Jesus, whom you are persecuting,' the Lord replied." Persecuting the church was tantamount to persecuting Jesus Himself. Far from doing the will of the Lord and doing Him a service, He had actually been destroying the Lord's household. "He was the chief of sinners. He was without God, without Christ, without hope."[3]

16 "Now get up and stand on your feet. I have appeared to you to appoint you as a servant and as a witness of what you have seen and will see of me." Jesus asked Saul to rise up because He had some work for him. He appeared to Saul for a specific purpose—to appoint him as his minister (KJV) and witness. To be a minister is to act under the supervision of another. To be a minister of Jesus is to be His ambassador or representative. A minister is His servant (NIV). Jesus now was Paul's Master. To be a witness is to testify that something has taken place. To witness for Christ is to testify about His death, burial, resurrection, and ascension. A witness must be born again because you cannot testify what you have not experienced.

17,18 "I will rescue you from your own people and from the Gentiles. I am sending you to them to open their eyes and turn them from darkness to light, and from the power of Satan to God, so that they may receive forgiveness of sins and a place among those who are sanctified by faith in me." There are three major things Jesus was telling Paul in these two verses. First, Jesus knew that Paul would be persecuted and not be well received by his own people. He assured Paul that He would rescue him.

Second, Jesus was sending Paul to open the eyes of Jews and Gentiles so that they might be transferred from the kingdom of darkness into God's marvelous light (1 Peter 2:9). This is the essence of salvation. Sinners are being captured from the power of Satan and placed in God's kingdom. Thus, Saul was commissioned to take the gospel to the Jews and the Gentiles.

Third, Jesus wanted people to receive forgiveness of their sins and to be part of His kingdom. Forgiveness of sins is a major result of salvation (Romans 4:7,8; 8:33, 34). Those who receive forgiveness of their sins would have a place among the sanctified.

Paul's Missionary Activity

Verses 19-23: "So then, King Agrippa, I was not disobedient to the vision from heaven. ²⁰ First to those in Damascus, then to those in Jerusalem and in all Judea, and then to the Gentiles, I preached that they should repent and turn to God and demonstrate their repentance by their deeds. ²¹ That is why some Jews seized me in the temple courts and tried to kill me. ²² But God has helped me to this very day; so I stand here and testify to small and great alike. I am saying nothing beyond what the prophets and Moses said would happen— ²³ that the Messiah would suffer and, as the first to rise from the dead, would bring the message of light to his own people and to the Gentiles."

19 Paul constantly appealed to Agrippa directly as he presented his defense. "So then, King Agrippa, I was not disobedient to the vision from heaven." Paul (and we too) could only respond to his calling in only two ways—obedience and disobedience. Paul had been faithful and obedient to the vision he had on Damascus road. Obedience is crucial to the Christian living. To be obedient requires that we submit to God's authority and do what He tells us to do.

20 "First to those in Damascus, then to those in Jerusalem and in all Judea, and then to the Gentiles, I preached that they should repent and turn to God and demonstrate their repentance by their deeds." This verse summarizes Paul's ministry. Paul demonstrated his obedience by proclaiming Christ in Damascus, Jerusalem, Judea, and to the Gentiles. His message to all of them is the same: repentance. This was the same message John the Baptist and Jesus preached. Repentance is a change of mind that leads to a change in behavior. John Phillips said, *"Repentance is a change of mind, regeneration is a change of heart, redemption is a change of state. All are part of a genuine salvation, and all are wrought by Jesus Christ"*(italic his).[4] As John and Jesus did, Paul required that people should show their repentance by their deeds.

21 "That is why some Jews seized me in the temple courts and tried to kill me." It was the message of repentance that Paul preached that got him in trouble with his fellow Jews. Paul was in trouble because He obeyed the Lord. Paul's major sin in the eyes of the Jews was his preaching to the Gentiles and claiming that they were equal with the Jews in the community of faith. Out of jealousy and blindness of heart, the Jews wanted to kill him. And that is the reason he stood before Agrippa.

22,23 "But God has helped me to this very day; so I stand here and testify to small and great alike. I am saying nothing beyond what the prophets and Moses said would happen—that the Messiah would suffer and, as the first to rise from the dead, would bring the message of light to his own people and to the Gentiles." Because God was with Paul, He helped him. Paul attributed his achievements to the enabling power of the Lord.

Verse 23 is a summary of the gospel. Paul's message was not new; it was totally in alignment with what Moses and the prophets predicted would happen. The OT foretold that the Messiah would suffer (Psalms 22 and 69; Isaiah 53), would be raised from the dead (Psalm 16:10), and would proclaim the message of light to Jews and Gentiles (Isaiah 49:6).

NOTES

1. Derek Carlsen, *Faith & Courage: Commentary on Acts* (Arlington Heights, IL: Christian Liberty Press, 2000), p. 514.
2. John MacArthur, *The MacArthur New Testament Commentary: Acts 13-28* (Chicago, IL: Moody Publishers, 1996), p. 334.
3. John Phillips, *Exploring Acts* (Grand Rapids, MI: Kregel Publications, 1986), p. 480.
4. Ibid., p. 484.

CHAPTER 31

PAUL BEFORE AGRIPPA – PART 3

Acts 26:24-32

Paul is Charged with Madness

*Verses 24-26: At this point Festus interrupted Paul's defense. "You are out of your mind, Paul!" he shouted. "Your great learning is driving you insane."*25 *"I am not insane, most excellent Festus," Paul replied. "What I am saying is true and reasonable.* 26 *The king is familiar with these things, and I can speak freely to him. I am convinced that none of this has escaped his notice, because it was not done in a corner.*

24 At this point Festus interrupted Paul's defense. What Paul was saying was too much for Festus' rational capacity. Imagine a rabbi addressing someone who was not a student of Scripture. Festus could not understand the subtleties of the Jewish religion. "You are out of your mind, Paul!" he shouted. "Your great learning is driving you insane." Festus accused Paul of being mad. He wholeheartedly rejected the idea of resurrection. Paul must be laboring under strong delusion to say that one dead man was alive. He must be really crazy.

25,26 "I am not insane, most excellent Festus," Paul replied. "What I am saying is true and reasonable. The king is familiar with these things, and I can speak freely to him. I am convinced that none of this has escaped his notice, because it was not done in a corner." In reality, Paul was not insane. He was speaking the truth, with a sound mind.

The truth about Christ's life was well known. It was a known fact that Jesus had ministered in Palestine with spectacular miracles. His trial, crucifixion, death, and resurrection were also public knowledge. Paul was quite sure that King Agrippa was familiar with these things. He called the king to witness to the fact that he was not out of his mind.

Paul Appeals to Agrippa

Verses 27-29: King Agrippa, do you believe the prophets? I know you do." *[28] Then Agrippa said to Paul, "Do you think that in such a short time you can persuade me to be a Christian?"[29] Paul replied, "Short time or long—I pray to God that not only you but all who are listening to me today may become what I am, except for these chains."*

27 Paul somehow perceived that Agrippa's heart was touched. He boldly talked to King Agrippa directly: "King Agrippa, do you believe the prophets? I know you do." Before Agrippa could reply, Paul answered for him in the affirmative. Agrippa had been familiar with the Jewish Scriptures. He could not deny that he believed the prophets. If the king believed the prophets, then he must admit that Jesus was the Messiah.

28 Then Agrippa asked Paul, "Do you think that in such a short time you can persuade me to be a Christian?" King Agrippa refused to answer Paul's question. He was probably embarrassed by Paul's direct question in the presence of the powerful audience. Rather than answering the question, he asked his own question. He was on the edge of conversion. It is tragic to think of how close he came to the point of salvation. Like Agrippa, many like to debate the issues of the gospel but refuse to make a personal decision for Christ.

29 Paul replied, "Short time or long—I pray to God that not only you but all who are listening to me today may become what I am, except for these chains." Whether with a short or long explanation of the gospel, it makes no difference. He wished everyone listening to him could become a Christian, a follower of Christ, without wearing chains as a result. In spite of his pleas, none of the individuals before him were converted.

Festus and Agrippa Declare Paul's Innocence

Verses 30-32: The king rose, and with him the governor and Bernice and those sitting with them. ³¹ After they left the room, they began saying to one another, "This man is not doing anything that deserves death or imprisonment." ³² Agrippa said to Festus, "This man could have been set free if he had not appealed to Caesar."

30 King Agrippa decided that the meeting was now over. As he got up from his seat, he signaled the end of the proceedings. With him the governor and Bernice and those sitting with them arose. Before the session was over, Paul became the judge, while Festus and King Agrippa became the defendants. One by one the prominent, the powerful, and the rich made their decision and rose.

31 After they left the room, they began saying to one another, "This man is not doing anything that deserves death or imprisonment." They all knew there were no cogent charges against Paul. They all agreed that he had done nothing wrong deserving imprisonment, much less death. It is possible for the emperor Nero to see Paul's innocence and set him free.

32 Agrippa said to Festus, "This man could have been set free if he had not appealed to Caesar." In theory, Agrippa was right. Once he appealed to Caesar, the die was cast. The matter is out of the jurisdiction of Governor Festus and King Agrippa. No lower court could change the course of events. Some believe Paul made a mistake by appealing to Caesar, but God was in total control and working all things so that Paul could be in Rome, as He promised (Acts 23:11). At least, Paul would gain a safe trip to Rome. Or could he have reached Rome in other ways? "If God is for us, who can be against us?" (Romans 8:31, NKJV).

CHAPTER 32

PAUL'S JOURNEY TO ROME – PART 1

Acts 27:1-12

Setting Sail

Verses 1-6: When it was decided that we would sail for Italy, Paul and some other prisoners were handed over to a centurion named Julius, who belonged to the Imperial Regiment. ² We boarded a ship from Adramyttium about to sail for ports along the coast of the province of Asia, and we put out to sea. Aristarchus, a Macedonian from Thessalonica, was with us. ³ The next day we landed at Sidon; and Julius, in kindness to Paul, allowed him to go to his friends so they might provide for his needs. ⁴ From there we put out to sea again and passed to the lee of Cyprus because the winds were against us. ⁵ When we had sailed across the open sea off the coast of Cilicia and Pamphylia, we landed at Myra in Lycia. ⁶ There the centurion found an Alexandrian ship sailing for Italy and put us on board.

1 When it was decided that they would sail for Italy, Paul and some other prisoners were handed over to a centurion named Julius, who belonged to the Imperial Regiment. That decision was ordered by the Lord (Psalm 37:23). The use of "we" indicates that Luke joined Paul as he sailed for Italy. Luke had not included himself as part of Paul's company since Acts 21:8. Aristarchus, a Macedonian from Thessalonica, was also with Paul (v. 2). Paul and other prisoners were placed under the custody of a centurion, Julius. Throughout the journey, Julius treated Paul with favor and kindness. As Chuck Smith rightly said, "Whenever you meet a centurion in the Scriptures, he's always described in a positive light."[1]

2 They started the journey from Caesarea by boarding a ship from Adramyttium about to sail for ports along the coast of the province of Asia, and they put out to sea. No ship seemed to be available to transport the prisoners directly from Caesarea to Italy. Aristarchus, a Macedonian from Thessalonica, was with them. He was among the group of believers that traveled with Paul to Jerusalem (Acts 20:4). Luke and Aristarchus ministered to the apostle.

3 The next day they landed at Sidon, which was 67 miles north of Caesarea. Sidon was a rival of Tyre. Julius, in kindness to Paul, allowed him to go to his friends so they might provide for his needs. Julius trusted Paul enough that he gave him some freedom. He would have paid with his own life if he lost Paul. Paul probably received food, clothing and other necessities for the journey from his friends at Sidon. He also received the uplifting boost of Christian fellowship.

4 From Sidon to Myra, we put out to sea again and passed to the lee of Cyprus because the winds were against us. "To pass the lee of Cyprus" meant to sail to the north of it between the island and the mainland. The journey was getting difficult and dangerous due to strong westerly winds. A direct route from Sidon to Myra would have caused the ship to move south and west of Cyprus. This was the same route Paul took when returning from his third missionary journey.

5 After rounding Cyprus, the ship made its way through the open sea. When they had sailed across the open sea off the coast of Cilicia and Pamphylia, they landed at Myra in Lycia, the most southern part of Asia Minor (modern Turkey). When Lycia was a Roman province, Myra was its capital. These areas were familiar to Paul because he was from Cilicia. They disembarked at Myra.

6 There the centurion, Julius, found an Alexandrian ship bound for Italy. The large ship from Egypt was carrying grain to Italy, in addition to 276 passengers (vs. 37, 38). Since the ship was large enough to carry his company, the centurion did not waste time in transferring his men and prisoners on board. The westerly winds were still blowing and making it difficult for them to make much progress, however.

The Boisterous Voyage

Verses 7, 8: We made slow headway for many days and had difficulty arriving off Cnidus. When the wind did not allow us to hold our course, we sailed to the lee of Crete, opposite Salmone. ⁸ We moved along the coast with difficulty and came to a place called Fair Havens, near the town of Lasea.

7 They made slow headway for many days and had difficulty arriving off Cnidus because the winds continued to be contrary. Cnidus was about 130 miles from Myra. With a favorable wind, the distance could be covered in a day or two. When the wind did not allow them to hold their course, they sailed to the lee of Crete, opposite Salmone. It had been a rough journey, a portent of what lay ahead.

8 The journey continued, but with slow progress. They sailed around the coast of Crete with difficulty and finally anchored at a bay called Fair Havens, near the town of Lasea. Lasea was a small town and did not offer much in terms of accommodations. The seamen wanted to sail to Phoenix, which was a larger city. Phoenix was about 40 miles away. "A guiding principle of sailing was that it was *dangerous* from mid-September to mid-November and *disastrous* from mid-November to mid-February (italic his)."²

Paul Advises Waiting for Better Weather

Verses 9-12: Much time had been lost, and sailing had already become dangerous because by now it was after the Day of Atonement. So Paul warned them, ¹⁰ "Men, I can see that our voyage is going to be disastrous and bring great loss to ship and cargo, and to our own lives also." ¹¹ But the centurion, instead of listening to what Paul said, followed the advice of the pilot and of the owner of the ship. ¹² Since the harbor was unsuitable to winter in, the majority decided that we should sail on, hoping to reach Phoenix and winter there. This was a harbor in Crete, facing both southwest and northwest.

9,10 The ship spent some time in the Fair Havens bay. Much time had been lost, and sailing had already become dangerous because by now it was after the Day of Atonement, Yom Kippur. This occurred on the tenth day of the month of Tishri. Reference to the Day of Atonement makes it possible to set the time of the voyage as early October A.D. 59.

At this point, Paul could not help but speak up, even though he was a prisoner. He warned against sailing on but suggested to stay in Fair Haven. He warned against taking undue risks and pointed to the danger ahead. He said, "Men, I can see that our voyage is going to be disastrous and bring great loss to ship and cargo, and to our own lives also." Paul was a seasoned traveler. He had already suffered three shipwrecks and spoke from experience (2 Corinthians 11:25).

11 But the centurion, instead of listening to what Paul said, followed the advice of the pilot and the owner of the ship. To the centurion, the opinion of the professional pilot carried more weight than the advice of Paul. That is often the case. The opinion of the expert is often preferred to the voice of a believer in touch with God. In this case, it was understandable but regretful. Having been overruled by the opinion of the experts, Paul retired to his cabin and prayed that all might go well.

12 Since the harbor at Fair Havens was unsuitable to spend the winter in, the majority of those making decisions felt that they should sail on, hoping to reach Phoenix and winter there. This was a harbor in the island of Crete with a better port, facing both southwest and northwest—the directions towards which the winds blew. The majority could not be wrong, especially when the experts are included. As we will see, it was a disastrous decision.

NOTES

1. Chuck Smith, *The Book of Acts* (Costa Mesa, CA: The Word for Today, 2013), p. 409.
2. B. Bruce Barton et al., *Life Application Bible Commentary: Acts* (Carol Stream, IL: Tyndale House Publishers, 1999), p. 436.

CHAPTER 33

PAUL'S JOURNEY TO ROME – PART 2

Acts 27:13-26

The Voyage Continues

Verses 13,14: When a gentle south wind began to blow, they saw their opportunity; so they weighed anchor and sailed along the shore of Crete. *¹⁴ Before very long, a wind of hurricane force, called the Northeaster, swept down from the island.*

13 When a gentle south wind began to blow, they felt they had gotten the opportunity they were looking for. They were deceived by the south wind and thought they could manage another 40 miles. It is easy to assume a seemingly favorable circumstance as a deciding factor in decision making. A seemingly golden opportunity may be deceptive. So they weighed anchor and sailed along the shore of Crete. They left Fair Havens and headed for Phoenix.

14 Before very long, what Paul predicted came to pass. A wind of hurricane force, called the Northeaster, swept down from the island. This was hurricane season. They were caught in a storm of hurricane proportion. The sailors attempted to sail the ship into the land, but they could not because the wind was too strong. There were no harbors in sight, only the open sea. Under such conditions, they were helpless and hopeless.

The Ship in the Storm

Verses 15-20: The ship was caught by the storm and could not head into the wind; so we gave way to it and were driven along. [16] As we passed to the lee of a small island called Cauda, we were hardly able to make the lifeboat secure, [17] so the men hoisted it aboard. Then they passed ropes under the ship itself to hold it together. Because they were afraid they would run aground on the sandbars of Syrtis, they lowered the sea anchor and let the ship be driven along. [18] We took such a violent battering from the storm that the next day they began to throw the cargo overboard. [19] On the third day, they threw the ship's tackle overboard with their own hands. [20] When neither sun nor stars appeared for many days and the storm continued raging, we finally gave up all hope of being saved.

15 The ship was caught by the storm and could not head into the wind. The storm blew with such violence that they could not face it. So they gave way to it and were driven along. Ancient ships were unable to face storm, as modern yachts can. The ship was at the mercy of the storm, which drove it farther and farther off shore. They wished they had listened to Paul.

16 As they passed to the lee of a small island called Cauda, the crew members were hardly able to make the lifeboat secure. Cauda was a tiny island about 30 miles from Crete. With great difficulty, they managed to haul aboard their lifeboat there, which was usually towed behind the ship. In a stormy situation like this, the lifeboat was in danger of being dashed against the ship.

17 So the men hoisted it aboard. Then they passed ropes under the ship itself to hold it together. All they were doing was binding the ship together to avoid it being broken apart. Because they were afraid they would run aground on the sandbars of Syrtis, they lowered the sea anchor and let the ship be driven along by the wind. The sailors were afraid they would be driven onto Syrtis, the Greek name for two area of quickstands on the coast of Libya.

18 They took such a violent battering from the storm that the next day they began to jettison the cargo, i.e. throw the goods overboard to lighten the ship and keep it afloat. They started dumping some of the grain they had brought from Egypt. Taking this remedial action did not help either. One can imagine what people would do out of desperation to save their lives.

19 On the third day, the process of lightening the ship continued. Everyone was put to work. They threw the ship's tackle overboard with their own hands. They were desperate. The violent storm continued for several days and nights. They threw away as many parts of the ship's equipment as possible. That action did nothing to alleviate their desperate situation.

20 When neither sun nor stars appeared for many days and the storm continued raging, they could not figure out where they were. The inclement weather prevented any observation of the sun in the day or stars at night. They finally gave up all hope of being saved. The sailors had done all common sense and experience could suggest. Nothing came out of their efforts to save the ship and their lives. It takes mature faith to trust Christ in such circumstances.

Paul Encourages Fellow Passengers

Verses 21-26: After they had gone a long time without food, Paul stood up before them and said: "Men, you should have taken my advice not to sail from Crete; then you would have spared yourselves this damage and loss. ²² But now I urge you to keep up your courage, because not one of you will be lost; only the ship will be destroyed. ²³ Last night an angel of the God to whom I belong and whom I serve stood beside me ²⁴ and said, 'Do not be afraid, Paul. You must stand trial before Caesar; and God has graciously given you the lives of all who sail with you.' ²⁵ So keep up your courage, men, for I have faith in God that it will happen just as he told me. ²⁶ Nevertheless, we must run aground on some island."

21 It appeared that the passengers were seasick, panic-stricken, and depressed. They could not eat. In the midst of storm, appetites were poor. After they had gone a long time without food, Paul stood up before them and said: "Men, you should have taken my advice not to sail from Crete; then you would have spared yourselves this damage and loss." Had they listened to Paul, they would not have been in this difficult situation. All suffering and loss could have been avoided if they had let the ship stay in Fair Havens, as Paul had suggested.

22 But Paul's purpose was not to make them feel bad for not taking his advice. He urged and encouraged them to keep up their courage, because not one of them would be lost; only the ship would be destroyed. Paul believed although the storm would claim the ship, nobody would lose his life. "When you've given up all hope and you're staring death in the face, you pay attention to someone holding out hope to you."[1]

23,24 Paul backed up his encouragement with a word from God. "Last night an angel of the God to whom I belong and whom I serve stood beside me and said, 'Do not be afraid, Paul. You must stand trial before Caesar; and God has graciously given you the lives of all who sail with you.'" Paul did not hesitate to let them know who he was and whom he served. That was why he could be cheerful while others were depressed, and hopeful while others doubted.

An angel of God revealed what would happen to Paul. "Surely the Sovereign LORD does nothing without revealing his plan to his servants the prophets" (Amos 3:7). This was the third time it was recorded that God encouraged Paul (Acts 18:9,10; 23:11).

All the passengers would all be protected because of Paul. "Unbelievers have no idea how much they owe, in the mercy of God, to the presence of righteous men among them."[2] It seemed that Paul had been praying about the situation. God confirmed what He told Paul earlier (Acts 23:11).

25 Paul delivered a message of hope and comfort to his desperate shipmates. "So keep up your courage, men, for I have faith in God that it will happen just as he told me." Paul literally asked them to cheer up. He assured them, as the prophet of God, that his prediction would come to pass. He believed in God and was sure He would keep His promises. We can always rest on the promises of God.

26 Coupled with the word of encouragement was the bad news: "Nevertheless, we must run aground on some island." In other words, they would be shipwrecked on an island. God's hand seemed to be directing the ship to a particular island. Paul took charge of the situation at a time when nobody else knew what to do. He started as a prisoner, but ended up being the captain. What a privilege to have someone like Paul in the storm-tossed ship.

NOTES

1. Chuck Smith, *The Book of Acts* (Costa Mesa, CA: The Word for Today, 2013), p. 415.
2. John MacArthur, *The MacArthur New Testament Commentary: Acts 13-28* (Chicago, IL: Moody Publishers, 1996), p. 351.

CHAPTER 34

PAUL'S JOURNEY TO ROME – PART 3

Acts 27:27-44

The Voyage Continues

Verses 27-30: On the fourteenth night we were still being driven across the Adriatic Sea, when about midnight the sailors sensed they were approaching land. [28] They took soundings and found that the water was a hundred and twenty feet deep. A short time later they took soundings again and found it was ninety feet deep. [29] Fearing that we would be dashed against the rocks, they dropped four anchors from the stern and prayed for daylight. [30] In an attempt to escape from the ship, the sailors let the lifeboat down into the sea, pretending they were going to lower some anchors from the bow.

27 On the fourteenth night after their departure from Fair Havens, they were still being driven across the Adriatic Sea. The Adriatic Sea was the sea between Italy to the west and Macedonia to the east. "A ship of that size with a drift of about 36 miles a day would take about two weeks to cover the 475 miles from Clauda to Malta."[1] About midnight the sailors sensed they were approaching land. Because of the storm, the sailors could hardly navigate.

28 To confirm what they sensed, the sailors took soundings and found that the water was 120 feet deep. This involved suspending a weight attached to a rope. How deep the weight went was an indication of how far the ship was from the sea bed. A short time later they took soundings again and found it was 90 feet deep. That indicated that the water was getting shallower and they were getting close to the shore.

29 Since they sensed they were close to land, they took some safety measures. They were afraid that they would soon be dashed against the rocks. They dropped four anchors from the stern. The four anchors should be able to hold the ship in position. It was night and they could not see anything. Out of desperation, they fervently prayed for daylight.

30 The anxious waiting was interrupted by the sailors' attempt to save their lives. They could not wait any longer. In an attempt to escape from the ship, the sailors let the lifeboat down into the sea. They tried to save the lifeboat earlier. They pretended they were going to lower some anchors from the bow. Their real motive was to save themselves using the lifeboat and leave others in the ship to perish.

Paul's Caution and Example

Verses 31-38: Then Paul said to the centurion and the soldiers, "Unless these men stay with the ship, you cannot be saved." [32] So the soldiers cut the ropes that held the lifeboat and let it drift away. [33] Just before dawn Paul urged them all to eat. "For the last fourteen days," he said, "you have been in constant suspense and have gone without food—you haven't eaten anything. [34] Now I urge you to take some food. You need it to survive. Not one of you will lose a single hair from his head." [35] After he said this, he took some bread and gave thanks to God in front of them all. Then he broke it and began to eat. [36] They were all encouraged and ate some food themselves. [37] Altogether there were 276 of us on board. [38] When they had eaten as much as they wanted, they lightened the ship by throwing the grain into the sea.

31 Paul saw through the game the sailors were trying to play and spoke up. He somehow knew what was going on through either experience or a special revelation from the Lord. He said to the centurion and the soldiers, "Unless these men stay with the ship, you cannot be saved." Paul, the prisoner, had taken command of the situation. God's promise does not negate our responsibility. Hearing from God does not excuse foolishness on our part.

32 The centurion, Julius, had learned his lesson. When Paul spoke, he responded positively. Taking Paul's word seriously, the centurion ordered the soldiers to cut the ropes that held the lifeboat and let it drift away. This way, the sailors could not escape. The ship was left to drift off.

33,34 Just before dawn Paul urged them all to eat. "For the last fourteen days," he said, "you have been in constant suspense and have gone without food—you haven't eaten anything. Now I urge you to take some food. You need it to survive. Not one of you will lose a single hair from his head." Going without food for 14 days, the people were physically weak. Paul insisted that they needed food to survive and make it to the shore. Swimming to safety would require strength. Faith never overlooks the practical details such as eating. If God's servants fail to take care of their bodies, their usefulness will be minimal.

35 After he said this, he took some bread and gave thanks to God in front of them all. Then he broke it and began to eat. In our home, we practice praying before meals. Paul was not parading his religion. He was not celebrating the Lord's Supper in the presence of unbelievers. He was a man of action. He was setting an example for other shipmates to follow. Exemplary living is the greatest influence we can make on others around us.

36 They were all encouraged by Paul's eating and ate some food themselves. It is amazing how a positive attitude can affect others. As Albert Schweitzer rightly said, "Example is not the main thing influencing others—it is the only thing." Paul later wrote Timothy to "set an example for the believers in speech, in life, in love, in faith, and in purity" (1 Timothy 4:12).

37 "Altogether there were 276 of us on board." Some have regarded this to be "triangular number" since it is the sum of the numbers 1 through 23. The number also shows that the ship was large. "Apparently there were four classes on board the ship; namely (1) the officials, including the captain, the pilot, and the centurion; (2) sailors; (3) soldiers; (4) prisoners."[2] We only know two of them by name—Julius the centurion and Paul the prisoner.

38 When they had eaten as much as they wanted, they lightened the ship by throwing the grain into the sea. They threw the remaining wheat overboard. Everything that was not important was jettisoned so that the ship might be lightened. By lightening the ship, it would be able to ride as high as possible. It would help them to come closer to the shore before it ran aground.

The Shipwreck

Verses 39-41: When daylight came, they did not recognize the land, but they saw a bay with a sandy beach, where they decided to run the ship aground if they could. ⁴⁰ Cutting loose the anchors, they left them in the sea and at the same time untied the ropes that held the rudders. Then they hoisted the foresail to the wind and made for the beach. ⁴¹ But the ship struck a sandbar and ran aground. The bow stuck fast and would not move, and the stern was broken to pieces by the pounding of the surf.

39 When daylight came, the sailors, the officers and the centurion could not recognize the land. The sailors had no idea of where they were. They later recognized the place to be Malta. "Malta" was a Phoenician name that means "refuge." They saw a bay with a sandy beach, where they decided to run the ship aground if they could. The pilot made every effort to get the ship to the beach.

40 The sailors were preparing to beach the ship. They were cutting loose the anchors and eliminating any kind of "breaking action." They left the anchors in the sea and at the same time untied the ropes that held the rudders. Then they hoisted the foresail to the wind and made for the beach. Their intension was to maneuver the ship towards the shore.

41 Before reaching land, the ship struck a sandbar and ran aground. The bow stuck fast and would not move, and the stern was broken to pieces by the pounding of the waves. The ship had to be abandoned. The traditional site for the shipwreck was St Paul's Bay, on the island of Malta.

All Reach Land Safely

Verses 42-44: The soldiers planned to kill the prisoners to prevent any of them from swimming away and escaping. ⁴³ But the centurion wanted to spare Paul's life and kept them from carrying out their plan. He ordered those who could swim to jump overboard first and get to land. ⁴⁴ The rest were to get there on planks or on other pieces of the ship. In this way everyone reached land safely.

42 The soldiers planned to kill the prisoners to prevent any of them from swimming away and escaping. They realized that they were personally responsible for the prisoners and their escape meant death for them. They were charged with the keeping and delivering of the prisoners. A Roman soldier could lose his life if he lost even just one prisoner. It was therefore natural that they would rather execute the prisoners there and then.

43 But the centurion disagreed with the soldiers. The centurion wanted to spare Paul's life at all costs and kept the soldiers from carrying out their plan despite the potential risk. He had come to respect and value Paul. Rather than killing the prisoners, he ordered those who could swim to jump overboard first and get to land.

44 The rest who could not swim found some practical means. The large ship had broken into pieces. The rest of the passengers were to get on planks or on other pieces of the ship. The evacuation plan worked since every one of the 276 passengers reached land safely—just as God promised. Despite the fear, fasting, loss of cargo, and wrecked ship, God was still in control. He would continue to be with Paul.

Map of Paul's journey under arrest from Palestine to Rome.
Source: https://www.ccel.org/bible/phillips/CN092MAPS1.htm

NOTES

1. John Phillips, *Exploring Acts* (Grand Rapids, MI: Kregel Publications, 1986), p. 508.
2. H. Leo Boles, *Acts* (Nashville, TN: Gospel Advocate Co., 1989), p. 424.
3. B. Bruce Barton et al., *Life Application Bible Commentary: Acts* (Carol Stream, IL: Tyndale House Publishers, 1999), p. 443.

CHAPTER 35

PAUL'S JOURNEY TO ROME – PART 4

Acts 28:1-10

Landing on Malta

Verses 1,2: Once safely on shore, we found out that the island was called Malta. ² The islanders showed us unusual kindness. They built a fire and welcomed us all because it was raining and cold.

1 After the 276 passengers arrived safely on shore, they found out that the island was called Malta. Malta was located about 60 miles south of Sicily and 320 miles from Rome. It was inhabited by Phoenician settlers. The name Malta in Phoenician dialect means "a place of refuge." The island lived up to its name. It got its independence from Britain in 1964.

2 The islanders showed them unusual kindness, beyond their expectation. They built a fire and welcomed them all because it was raining and cold. The survivors were fortunate to have been in the island with kind and hospitable folk. God went ahead of Paul and other passengers and prepared the way. God expects us to cultivate the habit of hospitality, especially to strangers (Romans 12:13).

A Viper Fastens on Paul's Hands

Verses 3-6: Paul gathered a pile of brushwood and, as he put it on the fire, a viper, driven out by the heat, fastened itself on his hand. ⁴ When the islanders saw the snake hanging from his hand, they said to each other, "This man must be a murderer; for though he escaped from the sea, the goddess Justice has not allowed him to live." [5] *But Paul shook the snake off into the fire and suffered no ill effects.* [6] *The people expected him to swell up or suddenly fall dead; but after waiting a long time and seeing nothing unusual happen to him, they changed their minds and said he was a god.*

3 Since more wood was needed to keep the fire burning, Paul made himself useful. He humbly went to fetch some wood for the benefit of others. He gathered a pile of brushwood and, as he put it on the fire, a viper (venomous snake), driven out by the heat, fastened itself on his hand. Scholars have debated what kind of snake this was, whether it was poisonous or not, and whether it actually bit Paul or not.

4 When the islanders saw the snake hanging from his hand, they had a ready-made explanation. They said to each other, "This man must be a murderer; for though he escaped from the sea, the goddess Justice has not allowed him to live." The islanders interpreted it as a judgment and concluded that Paul must be a criminal or a murderer, whom justice pursued. Nemesis (the goddess of divine retribution) was after Paul.

5 Paul must have smiled when he heard them. He knew the viper could not harm him. Paul shook the snake off into the fire and suffered no ill effects. Time passed but nothing happened to Paul. As the prophet Isaiah said, "No weapon forged against you will prevail, and you will refute every tongue that accuses you. This is the heritage of the servants of the LORD, and this is their vindication from me" (Isaiah 54:17).

6 The people expected him to swell up or suddenly fall dead. But after waiting and watching Paul a long time and seeing nothing unusual happen to him, they changed their minds and said he was a god. They no longer regarded Paul as a victim of their goddess Justice but a god himself. People can be fickle. This was the second time Paul would be regarded as a god (Acts 14:11). He soon dispelled the idea and proved to them that he was a human being like them.

Paul Heals Many

Verses 7-10: There was an estate nearby that belonged to Publius, the chief official of the island. He welcomed us to his home and showed us generous hospitality for three days. ⁸ His father was sick in bed, suffering from fever and dysentery. Paul went in to see him and, after prayer, placed his hands on him and healed him. ⁹ When this had happened, the rest of the sick on the island came and were cured. ¹⁰ They honored us in many ways; and when we were ready to sail, they furnished us with the supplies we needed.

7 "A second story about Paul's stay in Malta follows (verses 7-10). It is a miracle story, of the same kind as is related in the Gospels..."[1] There was an estate (lands, properties) nearby that belonged to Publius, the chief official (or Roman governor) of the island. Publius had an estate close to the site of the shipwreck. He was apparently wealthy. He welcomed us to his home and showed us generous hospitality for three days. That was not a small undertaking for 276 people.

8 Publius' father was sick in bed, suffering from a fever and dysentery. The gastric fever is known to be due to microbes in the milk of Maltese goats. Paul went in to see the sick man. After prayer, he placed his hands on him and healed him. The healing was instantaneous and complete. God rewarded the kindness of Publius to His people by healing his father. He is no man's debtor.

9 When this had happened, the news spread swiftly through the island. The rest of the sick on the island came to Paul for healing and were cured. This provided a great door of ministry for Paul. Paul was simply manifesting the gift of healing and authenticating his gospel message. Since they spent three months there (v. 11), Paul must have had several opportunities to preach the gospel to the Maltese.

10 They honored us in many ways. The people were grateful and they showed their appreciation in many ways. When we were ready to sail, they furnished us with the supplies we needed for the voyage. Because of Paul's ministry to the Maltese, the people gave them generous gifts and supplies they needed to complete their voyage of 320 miles to Rome. We remember that they lost everything due to the shipwreck.

NOTES

1. I. Howard Marshall, *Acts: Tyndale New Testament Commentaries* (Downers Grove, IL: InterVarsity Press, 1980), p. 438.

CHAPTER 36

PAUL ARRIVES IN ROME

Acts 28:11-16

The Voyage Resumes

Verses 11-14: After three months we put out to sea in a ship that had wintered in the island—it was an Alexandrian ship with the figurehead of the twin gods Castor and Pollux. ¹² We put in at Syracuse and stayed there three days. ¹³ From there we set sail and arrived at Rhegium. The next day the south wind came up, and on the following day we reached Puteoli. ¹⁴ There we found some brothers and sisters who invited us to spend a week with them. And so we came to Rome.

11 After staying in Malta for three months for the winter, they put out to sea in a ship that had wintered in the island. Ships started sailing between mid-February and mid-March. It was an Alexandrian ship with the figurehead of the twin gods Castor and Pollux. According to Greek mythology, the twin gods were sons of Zeus. Pagan Greeks commonly considered the twin gods as patrons and protectors of sailors. The captain of the ship was possibly more prudent and fortunate than the captain of the shipwrecked ship.

12 After leaving Malta, the ship sailed northeast to reach Syracuse. This was a direct course. Their first stop was at Syracuse, the capital of Sicily. That journey from Malta to Syracuse was about 90 miles and probably took a day. Syracuse was founded in 734 B.C. as a colony of Corinth. They stayed there for three days waiting for a favorable wind.

13 From Syracuse, they set sail and arrived at Rhegium. The next day the south wind came up, and on the following day we reached Puteoli (the modern Pozzuoli), the most important commercial seaport in Italy. Puteoli was located about 150 miles from Rome; it was the port of Rome. This last leg of Paul's voyage was smooth sailing; they received a warm reception from the people they encountered.

14 At Puteoli, the centurion allowed Paul the freedom to seek brethren. Paul and his companions found some brothers and sisters who invited them to spend a week with them. They felt at home among the brethren. Paul's name was now a household word everywhere by now. It must have been a wonderful week for Paul and the residents of Puteoli. And so they finally arrived at Rome.

Paul Welcomed to Rome

Verses 15,16: The brothers and sisters there had heard that we were coming, and they traveled as far as the Forum of Appius and the Three Taverns to meet us. At the sight of these people Paul thanked God and was encouraged. *[16] When we got to Rome, Paul was allowed to live by himself, with a soldier to guard him.*

15 The brothers and sisters there had heard that we were coming, and they traveled as far as the Forum of Appius and the Three Taverns to meet us. At the sight of these people Paul thanked God and was encouraged. Shared love has a way of encouraging people.

16 When they got to Rome, Paul was given some preferential treatment because he was a Roman citizen and had proved himself as a man of integrity who loved the Lord. Paul was allowed to live by himself, with a Roman soldier to guard him. A rotation of such soldiers watched over Paul 24/7.

CHAPTER 37

PAUL PREACHES IN ROME

Acts 28:17-32

Paul Calls the Jewish Leaders at Rome

Verses 17-22: Three days later he called together the local Jewish leaders. When they had assembled, Paul said to them: "My brothers, although I have done nothing against our people or against the customs of our ancestors, I was arrested in Jerusalem and handed over to the Romans. ¹⁸ They examined me and wanted to release me, because I was not guilty of any crime deserving death. ¹⁹ The Jews objected, so I was compelled to make an appeal to Caesar. I certainly did not intend to bring any charge against my own people. ²⁰ For this reason I have asked to see you and talk with you. It is because of the hope of Israel that I am bound with this chain."²¹ They replied, "We have not received any letters from Judea concerning you, and none of our people who have come from there has reported or said anything bad about you. ²² But we want to hear what your views are, for we know that people everywhere are talking against this sect."

17 Being a man of action, Paul could only rest for more than three days before meeting his fellow Jews. Perhaps it took three days to arrange an accommodation for Paul. One would assume that Paul would have no dealings with the Jews who persecuted him and caused his imprisonment. This was not the case with Paul. He must share the gospel. The kingdom business was urgent to him. Nothing could keep Paul silent.

Three days after he arrived in Rome, he called together the local Jewish leaders on short notice. Paul was still following his strategy of first approaching the Jewish community whenever he arrived in a city. When the Jewish leaders had assembled, Paul said to them: "My brothers, although I have done nothing against our people or against the customs of our ancestors, I was arrested in Jerusalem and handed over to the Romans." Paul asserted his innocence. He did not commit any crime against the Jews or their customs.

18 When the Romans examined Paul, they wanted to release him, because he was not guilty of any crime deserving death. Governors Felix and Festus and King Agrippa all confirmed that Paul was innocent of the charges against him and they were unwilling to execute him. The charges against him could not be substantiated. They could have released Paul had the Jews not objected.

19 The adamant objections of the Jews compelled Paul to make an appeal to Caesar. In other words, the reason Paul appealed to Caesar was that the Jews objected to the Roman's desire to set him free. Paul had to appeal to Caesar in order to save his life. He certainly did not intend to bring any charge against his own people. He did not want to be an instrument in the hands of Roman tyranny against his people.

20 "For this reason I have asked to see you and talk with you. It is because of the hope of Israel that I am bound with this chain." The ancestral hope of Israel was the Messiah. He was hated by his countrymen because he proclaimed that Jesus was the Messiah. Paul was in chains because he believed that the Messiah had come and all over the world Jews and Gentiles were entering into His kingdom.

Paul left much unsaid because this was just an introductory meeting. The purpose of the meeting was to get acquainted with each other.

21 They replied, "We have not received any letters from Judea concerning you, and none of our people who have come from there has reported or said anything bad about you." They denied all knowledge of any incidence involving Paul either through letter writing or through a messenger from Judea. They had not received any communication about Paul from church leaders in Jerusalem.

22 They expressed their desire to hear what Paul's views were. They knew that people everywhere were talking against this sect or this new movement. Although they were not familiar with Paul's case, they knew about Christianity. The church of Christ was already growing in Rome and the Jewish leaders were familiar with it. But the Jewish leaders had heard nothing good about the sect to which Paul belonged.

Paul Preaches to the Jews

Verses 23-29: They arranged to meet Paul on a certain day, and came in even larger numbers to the place where he was staying. He witnessed to them from morning till evening, explaining about the kingdom of God, and from the Law of Moses and from the Prophets he tried to persuade them about Jesus. [24] Some were convinced by what he said, but others would not believe. [25] They disagreed among themselves and began to leave after Paul had made this final statement: "The Holy Spirit spoke the truth to your ancestors when he said through Isaiah the prophet:

[26] "'Go to this people and say,
"You will be ever hearing but never understanding;
* you will be ever seeing but never perceiving."*
[27] For this people's heart has become calloused;
* they hardly hear with their ears,*
* and they have closed their eyes.*
Otherwise they might see with their eyes,
* hear with their ears,*
* understand with their hearts*
* and turn, and I would heal them.'*

[28] "Therefore I want you to know that God's salvation has been sent to the Gentiles, and they will listen!"

23 At their first meeting, the Jewish showed interest in what Paul had to say. Since he was under house arrest, he could not go to the synagogues as usual. He summoned the Jewish leaders to his residence for the second meeting, which lasted the whole day. "They arranged to meet Paul on a certain day, and came in even larger numbers to the place where he was staying. He witnessed to them from morning till evening, explaining about the kingdom of God, and from the Law of Moses and from the Prophets he tried to persuade them about Jesus." Paul's theme was the kingdom of God. Using the Law and the Prophets, he provided some detailed explanation and confronted them with the need for accepting Jesus as the Messiah.

24 Paul's daylong exposition of the Scriptures split the Jewish leaders in two. Some were convinced by what Paul said, but others would not believe. As usual, people respond to the gospel differently. Some believed what they heard and responded in faith to Jesus Christ. Others rejected Paul's apostolic witness and turned their backs on the only way of salvation. Their unbelief was a choice. Whenever the gospel is preached, eternal issues are at stake. It is our duty to respond favorably to the gospel message. Failure to do so is direct disobedience to God.

25-27 After listening to Paul for the whole day, they disagreed among themselves and began to leave after Paul had made this final statement: "The Holy Spirit spoke the truth to your ancestors when he said through Isaiah the prophet: "Go to this people and say, 'You will be ever hearing but never understanding; you will be ever seeing but never perceiving. For this people's heart has become calloused; they hardly hear with their ears, and they have closed their eyes. Otherwise they might see with their eyes, hear with their ears, understand with their hearts and turn, and I would heal them.'""

Paul had the final word and it was a word of rebuke. He quoted Isaiah 6:9,10. This quotation was of spiritual significance to Israel. It appears seven times in the Bible (e.g. Matthew 13:14; Romans 11:8). It described Israel's tragic spiritual condition. The quotation draws a difference between hearing and listening, and between seeing and perceiving. It goes on to attribute our failure to comprehend to our hard hearts, deaf ears, and closed eyes. It is a solemn warning for those who play with the gospel.

28 "Therefore I want you to know that God's salvation has been sent to the Gentiles, and they will listen!" From now on, the Gentiles would be given the priority in receiving the gospel. Paul would focus his ministry on those who would embrace the gospel and give it a more favorable response. People living in hopeless conditions will receive the message of hope. The Gentiles will listen with open ears, while the Jews have closed theirs. The fact that Paul started to focus on the Gentiles does not mean that God has forsaken His people (Romans 11:1, 2).

29 Some manuscripts omit this verse: "After he said this, the Jews left, arguing vigorously among themselves." But it accurately reflects what happened to the Jewish leaders after Paul's long sermon.

Paul in Rome

Verses 30,31: For two whole years Paul stayed there in his own rented house and welcomed all who came to see him. ³¹ He proclaimed the kingdom of God and taught about the Lord Jesus Christ—with all boldness and without hindrance!

30 For two whole years Paul stayed there in his own rented house and welcomed all who came to see him. He was not idle. Despite being a prisoner under house arrest, Paul had the liberty to welcome visitors to his house. He did not have the freedom of going out, but he could receive visitors. The two-year delay in Paul's case was probably due to the backlog of cases. It was during this period that Paul wrote the so-called prison epistles—Philippians, Ephesians, Colossians, and Philemon. He himself hoped to be released soon (Philippians 1:23-27; 2:24) and most scholars believe that he was. "And the Pastoral Epistles supply evidence that he was, for he resumed his travels for about two more years before being re-arrested, re-tried, condemned and executed in AD 64."[1]

31 Although Paul remained in prison, confined to his rented house, he did not stop in reaching others with the gospel. The house became the international headquarters of global evangelism. Paul proclaimed the kingdom of God and taught about the Lord Jesus Christ—with all boldness and without hindrance! Paul could not be shut up. The gospel has reached our generation indicating that it cannot be stopped.

Luke has stressed throughout Acts that the Holy Spirit controls mission work. Although the Acts of the Apostles have finished, the Acts of the Holy Spirit continue.

NOTES

1. John R.W. Stott, *The Message of Acts* (Downers Grove, IL: IVP Academic, 1990), p. 405.

SELECTED BIBLIOGRAPHY

Adeyemo, Tokunboh (ed.), *Africa Bible Commentary* (Nairobi, Kenya: WordAlive Publishers, 2006).

Arnold, Clinton E., *Acts* (Grand Rapids, MI: Zondervan, 2002).

Barton, B. Bruce et al., *Life Application Bible Commentary: Acts* (Carol Stream, IL: Tyndale House Publishers, 1999).

Boles, H. Leo, *Acts* (Nashville, TN: Gospel Advocate Co., 1989).

Carlsen, Derek, *Faith & Courage: Commentary on Acts* (Arlington Heights, IL: Christian Liberty Press, 2000).

Fernando, Ajith, *Acts: The NIV Application Commentary* (Grand Rapids, MI: Zondervan, 1998).

Ger, Steven, *The Book of Acts: Witnesses to the World* (Chattanooga, TN: AMG Publishers, 2004).

Horton, Stanley M., *Acts: A Logion Press Commentary* (Springfield, MO: Logion Press, 2001).

Hughes, R. Kent, *Acts: The Church Afire* (Wheaton, IL: Crossway, 1996).

Kwon, Yon Gyong (ed.), *A Commentary on Acts* (Minneapolis, MN: Fortress Press, 2015).

MacArthur, John, *The MacArthur New Testament Commentary: Acts 13-28* (Chicago, IL: Moody Publishers, 1996).

Marshall, Howard I., *Acts: Tyndale New Testament Commentaries* (Downers Grove, IL: InterVarsity Press, 1980).

Milne, Bruce, *Acts: Witnesses to Him* (Fearn, Ross-shire, UK: Christian Focus Publications, 2010).

Ogilvie, Lloyd J., *Acts: The Communicator's Commentary* (Waco, TX: Word Books, 1983).

Phillips, John, *Exploring Acts* (Grand Rapids, MI: Kregel Publications, 1986).

Smith, Chuck, *The Book of Acts* (Costa Mesa, CA: The Word for Today, 2013).

Stott, John R. W., *The Message of Acts* (Downers Grove, IL: IVP Academic, 1990).

Thomas, Derek W. H., *Acts: Reformed Expository Commentary* (Phillipsburg, NJ: P&R Publishing Co., 2011).

Thompson, Richard P., *Acts: A Commentary in the Wesleyan Tradition* (Kansas City, KS: Beacon Hill Press, 2015).

Wagner, C. Peter, *The Book of Acts: A commentary* (Ventura, CA: Regal From Gospel Light, 2008).

Wiersbe, Warren W., *Be Daring: Acts 13-28* (Colorado Springs, CO: David C. Cook, 1988).

Williams, David J., *Acts: Understanding the Bible Commentary Series* (Grand Rapids, MI: Baker Books, 1990).

Willimon, William H., *Acts: Interpretation* (Louisville, KT: WJK Press, 1988).

INDEX

Printed in the United States
By Bookmasters